The Social Gospel of Jesus

The Social Gospel of Jesus

The Kingdom of God in Mediterranean Perspective

Bruce J. Malina

Fortress Press
Minneapolis

THE SOCIAL GOSPEL OF JESUS
The Kingdom of God in Mediterranean Perspective

Cover design: Marti Naughton
Book design: Ann Delgehausen
Cover art: Multiplication of Loaves and Fishes. Early Christian Mosaic. S. Apollinare Nuovo, Ravenna, Italy. SCALA/Art Resource N.Y. Used by permission.

Frontispiece: A lion on the Ishtar Gate from Babylon (c. 600 B.C.E.); Pergamon Museum, Berlin, Germany. Photo by K. C. Hanson. Used by permission. Pg. 14: Statue of the Roman emperor Tiberius; Pergamon Museum, Berlin, Germany. Photo by K. C. Hanson. Used by permission. Pg. 36: Miniature illuminated manuscript painting of the fall of Jerusalem in 70 C.E.; the Rhyming Bible by Jacob van Maerlant, 1332. Pg. 70: Roman funerary relief; Pergamon Museum, Berlin, Germany. Photo by K. C. Hanson. Used by permission. Pg. 96: Athenian tetradrachma from the Hellenistic period; the head of the helmeted Athena Parthenos (obverse); an owl standing on an amphora and the names of the mintmasters, surrounded by an olive branch (reverse); the coin is located in the Staatliche Museen, Berlin, Germany. Photo from Helmut Koester and Holland L. Hendrix, *Archaeological Resources for New Testament Study* (Philadelphia: Fortress Press). Used by permission. Pg. 112: Via Dolorosa, Jerusalem, the West Bank. Photo by K. C. Hanson. Used by permission. Pg. 140: Ancient steps leading from the western hill to the Kidron Valley to connect with the road to Gethsemane, Jerusalem, the West Bank. Photo by Thomas Hoffman, S.J. Used by permission.

Library of Congress Cataloging-in-Publication Data

Malina, Bruce J.
     The social gospel of Jesus : the kingdom of God in Mediterranean perspective /
Bruce J. Malina
               p.   cm.
     Includes bibliographical references and indexes.
     ISBN 0-8006-3247-8 (alk. paper)
            1. Kingdom of God—Biblical teaching. 2. Bible. N.T.—Social scientific criticism. 3. Social gospel. 4. Mediterranean Region—Social conditions. I. Title.

BS2417.K5 M29 2000
231.7'2'09012—dc21   00-061749

Manufactured in the U.S.A.   AF 1-3247

06   05   04   03   02   01   1   2   3   4   5   6   7   8   9   10

For

Jerry H. Neyrey, S.J.

FELLOW CARDIOPHILE,

CONGENIAL COLLEAGUE,

INSIGHTFUL COLLABORATOR,

ASSIDUOUS STUDENT OF THE WORD OF GOD

CONTENTS

Foreword

Very few scholars are given the opportunity to make fundamental changes in their field of study and, when presented with such an opportunity, even fewer have the courage and fortitude it takes to introduce such change.[1] Pioneers in any academic endeavor must contend with entrenched principalities and powers, well-established methods, and the so-called "assured results" of previous study. This is as true of biblical studies as it is of other academic endeavors. Scholarship is, in many ways, resistant to change, and scholars often resent innovation in their fields of study.

It is a tribute to Bruce Malina's character, creativity, and cussed perseverance that, when he was provided with such an opportunity, he took it, and New Testament studies have not been the same. When he published *The New Testament World: Insights from Cultural Anthropology* (1981, rev. ed. 1993), he made a significant contribution to a paradigm shift in biblical studies. In this role, he was part of a pioneering group of scholars, including Richard L. Rohrbaugh (*The Biblical Interpreter*, 1978), Gerd Theissen (*Sociology of Early Palestinian Christianity*, 1978), Norman K. Gottwald (*The Tribes of Yahweh*, 1979), and John H. Elliott (*A Home for the Homeless*, 1981),[2] all of whom were discovering and exploring the possibilities of using the social sciences to interpret biblical texts and to reconstruct the world in which those texts were written. By the mid-1980s, two volumes of *Semeia* (35 and 37) were devoted to this new "social-scientific criticism" of the New Testament and the Hebrew Bible and, by the end of the decade, social-scientific criticism had found a place in biblical studies.

In furthering this project, Malina's productivity has been truly remarkable. He has written monographs on a wide variety of subjects, including an application of the work of Mary Douglas to biblical studies,[3] a study of the book of Revelation,[4] and collections of essays on specific themes and topics related to the study of the historical Jesus and the Gospels.[5] In addition to these studies, he has written articles too numerous to mention, illuminating specific issues in the biblical world in the light of the social sciences. Many of them are mentioned in the bibliography found at the end of this present study. But Bruce Malina is more than an isolated scholar; he is a leading voice in a movement in biblical studies, and he has conducted himself accordingly. He has, for example, worked cooperatively with a number of colleagues. His collaborative work includes two commentaries written with Richard L. Rohrbaugh,[6] two studies co-authored with Jerome H. Neyrey, and a handbook co-edited with John J. Pilch.[8] This commitment to collegial and collaborative work has marked Bruce's scholarly career, and it has placed a distinctive stamp on the field of New Testament studies. To encourage cooperative work among biblical scholars using the social sciences, Malina helped to form "The Context Group," a gathering of scholars that meets to provide peer reviews of works in progress and to facilitate sharing of research and bibliographic resources. In this setting, Malina has generously encouraged the work of younger scholars.

I first heard of Bruce through one of his students who came to the seminary in Berkeley where I was then teaching. When the student took my New Testament Introduction course, he seemed to be extremely well versed in the New Testament world and, when I asked him how he had gained so much knowledge, he began to praise one of his undergraduate religion teachers at Creighton University. I had never heard of Bruce Malina, but, at the student's urging, I arranged for him to do a lecture at the Graduate Theological Union in Berkeley. He was an immediate success. His first lecture changed the way I would approach the New Testament, and I have never seen it the same way again.

At a recent meeting of a scholarly society, Bruce and I were talking about projects on which we were engaged when a colleague came up to greet him. "What are you working on these days?" she asked. Bruce paused for a moment and said, "I'm just doing Bible study. That's all. Just doing Bible study." After a moment of embarrassed silence, the colleague faded back into the crowd, no doubt thinking that Bruce had taken leave of his senses. At the time, I thought he was making an impertinent remark; but I have had time to reconsider. If one of the fundamental tasks of biblical interpretation is to understand the biblical text in its own world, then Malina is truly engaged in Bible study at its most basic level. The chapters in this volume illustrate the point quite well. Jesus' proclamation of the kingdom of God has a scholarly history that, in shorter historical perspective, spans the twentieth century. But rarely have the participants in the discussion asked the most basic of questions: What would it mean to ancient Mediterranean peoples to hear such a proclamation? What would the phrase "the kingdom of God" mean to an ancient Mediterranean person? Malina begins his study of the Bible by asking just such basic questions and, because he asks what seem to be the most obvious questions, even though they have been overlooked or ignored as unimportant, his study will change the way we view biblical texts and the world of the Bible.

Malina's work embodies a paradox. It is only when we place biblical texts in their own world that they are freed to speak to ours, for the kind of study that Malina does prevents us from projecting our world onto the biblical world, thereby depriving it of the opportunity to speak its own distinctive, strange, and even alien "word" to us. This is why Malina has not been hesitant to criticize "the received view" and identify "what it cannot do."⁹ His project has been to deconstruct as well as reconstruct an approach to biblical studies.

It is, therefore, appropriate to conclude this Foreword with an invitation and a warning. If you would like to see Jesus' proclamation of the kingdom of God in a new, refreshing, and unconventional way, please read on. But beware! You will never see the Bible in the same way again. That is the gift and challenge of Bruce Malina's scholarly career.

—WILLIAM R. HERZOG II

1. This foreword is based on remarks made to the Colgate Rochester Divinity School/Crozer Theological Seminary community when Malina came to deliver the 1999 Walter Rauschenbusch Lectures. It was my pleasant duty to introduce Bruce and his work.

2. The publishing information is as follows: Bruce J. Malina, *The New Testament World: Insights from Cultural Anthropology* (Atlanta: John Knox, 1981; rev. ed., Louisville: Westminster John Knox, 1993); Richard L. Rohrbaugh, *The Biblical Interpreter: An Agrarian Bible in An Industrial Age* (Philadelphia: Fortress Press, 1978); Gerd Theissen, *Sociology of Early Palestinian Christianity* (Philadelphia: Fortress Press, 1978); Norman K. Gottwald, *The Tribes of Yahweh: A Sociology of the Religion of Liberated Israel, 1250–1050 B.C.E.* (Maryknoll: Orbis, 1979); and John H. Elliott, *A Home for the Homeless: A Sociological Exegesis of I Peter, Its Situation and Strategy* (Minneapolis: Fortress Press, 1981; 1990). The issues of *Semeia* are: John H. Elliott, ed. *Semeia 35: Social-Scientific Criticism of the New Testament and Its Social World* (1986); Norman K. Gottwald, ed. *Semeia 37:*

Social-Scientific Criticism of the Hebrew Bible and Its Social World: The Israelite Monarchy (1986).

3. Bruce J. Malina, *Christian Origins and Cultural Anthropology: Practical Models for Biblical Interpretation* (Atlanta: John Knox, 1986).

4. Bruce J. Malina, *On the Genre and Message of Revelation: Star Visions and Sky Journeys* (Peabody: Hendrickson, 1995).

5. Bruce J. Malina, *The Social World of Jesus and the Gospels* (New York: Routledge, 1996).

6. Bruce J. Malina and Richard L. Rohrbaugh, *Social-Science Commentary on the Synoptic Gospels* (Minneapolis: Fortress Press, 1992); idem, *Social-Science Commentary on the Gospel of John* (Minneapolis: Fortress Press, 1998).

7. Bruce J. Malina and Jerome H. Neyrey, *Calling Jesus Names: The Social Value of Labels in Matthew* (Sonoma, Calif.: Polebridge, 1988); idem., *Portraits of Paul: An Archaeology of Ancient Personality* (Louisville: Westminster John Knox, 1996).

8. John J. Pilch and Bruce J. Malina, *Biblical Social Values and Their Meaning: A Handbook* (Peabody: Hendrickson, 1993; rev. ed. 1998).

9. See his essay, "The Received View and What It Cannot Do: III John and Hospitality," in Bruce J. Malina, *The Social World of Jesus and the Gospels*, 217–41.

PREFACE

The chapters that follow represent expanded versions of the Rauschenbusch Lectures for 1999 delivered at the Colgate-Rochester Divinity School. Walter Rauschenbusch was much interested in the social gospel. The word "social" had much the same meaning as Europeans shared when they spoke of the "social question." Pope Leo XIII, for example, in his great encyclical Providentissimus Deus, addressed the "social question" at length. At the time, "social" was a code word for the poor and for the poverty they endured due to the great transformation known as the Industrial Revolution (see Malina and Rohrbaugh 1992: 1–13). People were displaced, dispossessed, off-centered, and forced into inhumane ways of living. Rauschenbusch was devoted to marshaling the forces of American Christianity in the service of the social gospel with a view to ameliorating the lot of the poor. In this context I thought it fitting to consider Jesus' social gospel. First-century problems, however, were quite different from early twentieth-century problems. Jesus' social gospel—his message and proclamation from God for Israel's off-centered populations—was not rooted in any Industrial Revolution. Rather, it germinated in the larger matrix of the political order centered on the Roman emperors and their elite networks. With a view to understanding the significance of Jesus' political gospel in his time and his place as well as to elucidating the aftermath of his proclamation and activity, I offer the follow chapters.

With this publication, I wish to thank the President of Colgate Rochester, James H. Evans Jr., and the Vice President for Academic Life and Dean of Faculty, William R. Herzog II, along with the faculty, alumni, and local clergy who made the occasion a truly memorable one.

INTRODUCTION

I think even the most skeptical historian would agree that if Jesus spoke about anything, he spoke about the kingdom of heaven (see Willis 1987; Chilton 1994; Fuellenbach 1995). The burden of Jesus' proclamation was the kingdom of heaven, a politically correct, Israelite way of saying "kingdom of God." The question I wish to address in this book is: To what sort of social problem was Jesus' proclamation of the kingdom of God meant to be a solution? The word "kingdom" by any estimation is a word describing a society's political institution. It is, in origin, a political term, even if a number of Bible readers, professional and nonprofessional, have appropriated the term metaphorically. What did a phrase like "kingdom of God" mean to Jesus' Israelite audience in the first century? The proclamation of the kingdom of God meant at least that the God of Israel would be taking over control of the country soon. The phrase "kingdom of God" is a descriptive and concrete way of saying "theocracy." Theocracy is a political science term referring to the political system of societies claiming to be ruled by God. Iran is a contemporary example.

The outcome of Jesus' career makes it rather certain that his proclamation of the kingdom of God was political, not metaphorical, much less "spiritual," whatever that nineteenth-century word might mean. In what sort of first-century Mediterranean social context would the proclamation of theocracy make sense? In all gospel accounts about Jesus' proclamation of the kingdom, no one asks for an explanation. While Jesus was reported to have offered a range of descriptions of what God's rule is like (kingdom parables), he never explained what the structure of this kingdom of God might be, who would constitute its personnel, its bureaucracy, its chief executive. Why was there not more discussion about the structure and functions of the theocracy that Jesus proclaimed? About how such a theocracy might work in everyday life?

1

Why did people seem to know exactly what Jesus was referring to when he spoke about theocracy? It would seem that "kingdom of God" was another of the many high context terms mentioned in the New Testament. For the prevailing language "context" generally in vogue in the ancient Mediterranean was that of a high context society, as opposed to a low context society (see Hall 1976: 91–101; 1983: 59–77; Malina 1991a).

HIGH AND LOW CONTEXT SOCIETIES

Low context societies produce detailed verbal documents that spell out as much as possible, leaving little to the imagination. For example, most United States citizens know about the annual ritual of paying income taxes. Yet most do not know that the tax code contains some six thousand pages explaining the income tax. This points up the general norm of low context societies—namely, that most things must be clearly defined—hence, information must be continually added if meaning is to be constant. Such societies are fine-print societies, societies "of law," where every dimension of life must be described by legislators to make things lawful, even including, for example, twenty pages of detailed legal directions about how much fat is allowed in commercially sold sausage. The *Congressional Record*, a document produced by the United States government, offers hours of low context reading for whoever might wish to be entertained in this way. Hall considers the United States and northern European countries as typically low context societies.

High context societies produce sketchy and impressionistic documents, leaving much to the reader's or hearer's imagination and common knowledge. Since people living in these societies believe that few things have to be spelled out, few things are in fact spelled out. This is so because the people have been socialized into widely shared ways of perceiving and acting; therefore, much can be assumed. People in high context societies presume, for example, that helping out a person in dire need makes that person obligated for the rest of his or her life to the helper. There simply is no need to spell out all these obligations, as we would when we sign for a car loan. In high context societies, little new information is necessary for meaning to be constant. Hall lists the Mediterranean, among other areas, as populated with high context societies. Clearly the Bible—along with other writings from ancient Mediterranean peoples—fits this high context profile.

How different it is, then, for low context United States and northern European readers to read a high context document. To allay the difference, low context readers presume the high context documents are in fact other instances of the low context documents they are used to. The New Testament, for example, is believed to contain sufficient information to direct Christian living in any society! Attuned to detail, low context readers simply do not know what is assumed in a high context society. The purpose of historical biblical interpretation is to explain the assumptions underlying the high context documents that form the New Testament, assumptions that the authors of those documents shared with high context readers of their Mediterranean world.

It will help us understand Hall's observations about high and low context societies if we attend to their respective communication problems. The typical communication problem in low context societies such as the United States, for example, is giving people information they do not need, "talking down" to them by spelling out absolutely everything. Consider the endless amount of information printed by the U.S. Government Printing Office alone, or the useless knowledge that passes as news in the media. In contrast, the typical communication problem in high context societies is not giving people enough information, thus "mystifying" them. Consider the broad range of mystifications and hidden meanings derived from the Mediterranean, high context Bible by sincere and honest low context United States and northern European readers—from fundamentalist television preachers to learned literary critics.

Biblical mystifications and hidden meanings are contrived in a number of ways and for various reasons in our low context societies. A glance at the spate of "relevant" commentaries on Revelation is a case in point. So, too, the fate of the term "kingdom of God" in low context societies. The fact is, however, that "kingdom of God" comes from a high context society and is a high context term. High context terms are words and phrases referring to social realities with wide-ranging ramifications known to all persons in a given society. There is no need to spell out the details; everybody knows what is involved. Reference to the kingdom of God simply indicates the tip of some proverbial iceberg, as is normal with high context referents. What does that iceberg look like?

To understand the high context statements attributed to Jesus requires the same effort as understanding anyone from a different time and place. Communication by means of language takes place, as a rule, through the formulation, exchange, and interpretation of discrete units of meaning called "texts," extemporaneous or prepared. Texts differ from sentences that consist of a group of words expressing a complete thought. Sometimes it takes one thought to communicate one meaning (for example, "Keep off the grass"). But 99 percent of the time, human beings require many thoughts to communicate even simple meanings (for example, a philosophical essay on being). Instances of texts include television shows, news magazines, letters from the Internal Revenue Service requesting an audit, direct mail advertising addressed to "Occupant," or the sports pages in a daily newspaper. These do not require special efforts at interpretation because they are adequately low context for persons enculturated in the United States.

A felt need to interpret any form of communication implies that some information is lacking for an adequate understanding of a text or text-segment. Interpretation entails providing the requisite information so that a given text might be readily understood. To interpret means to make explicit and clear those features in a text that are implicit and unclear, and thus to facilitate effective communication. For example, what information about sheep and goats might be needed to make the parable in Matt 25:31-46 meaningful (for example, see Blok 1984)? Would the meanings ascribed to those animals in Idaho or Wyoming suffice to explain the meanings they carry in the Mediterranean today, much less in the first-century Mediterranean world? What about the meanings given those animals by present-day city dwellers who cannot even find a goat in the place they usually meet up with sheep—the local supermarket? Similarly, did marriage mean the same to a first-century Mediterranean person as it does to us? What about divorce in the New Testament: the dissolution of a Mediterranean marriage? And what about abstract values and social arrangements such as economics or politics, religion or kinship, or sin, peace, war, love, liberty, and individualism?

All persons who communicate with others carry on an interpretative enterprise. People carry around one or more models of how society works and how human beings interact. Such models serve as radar screens, constraining people to see certain things in their experience while blocking out the rest. In other words, individuals appropriate socially shared scenarios of how the world works, and these scenarios greatly influence what they look for in their experiences, what they actually see, and what they eventually do with their observations by way of fitting them into some larger framework of understanding. Such scenarios or models of the world and of persons in the world consist chiefly of: 1) structures or recurring patterns of how things go or happen or are constituted; and 2) values or assessments of worth and purpose (see Carney 1975).

One of the difficulties posed by reading the Bible is the large amount of high context, implicit information any reader in the United States would require to interpret what is being communicated. After all, what is being described in those documents derives from societies radically different from our own, both in structure and in core values. Furthermore, the documents come from radically different geographic settings and the concerns they address are situated some millennia in the past. If a text is a piece of language intended to communicate effectively, it should be fairly obvious that the contemporary reader can hardly be said to understand automatically what the biblical author is saying.

Patterns of language at a level higher than the sentence derive from the social system of the speaker or writer. We have language patterns such as food and movie advertisements and requests for bus tickets because of the way we buy and sell food, go to the movies, and ride buses. Without some understanding of the social system that gives rise to various patterns of speech, often called "literary forms" by biblical scholars, those patterns are misinterpreted (for example, a movie house called "A & P Supermarket" showing Round Steak at $1.99) or simply not understood. What I am suggesting is that the Bible is necessarily misunderstood if one's reading of it is not grounded in an appreciation of the social systems from which its documents arose. Furthermore, all the attitudes, values, and behavioral interactions described in the Bible are necessarily misunderstood—or are simply not understood—without some appreciation and understanding of the social system assumed and reflected in the biblical writings. Even such concrete items as house, courtyard, cup, sheep, and goat carry meanings lost to and/or replaced by the contemporary reader. The interpretive situation is even more hopeless regarding abstract values such as peace, wealth, poverty, humility, and love. A Bible reader who wishes to understand these terms is left with the option of reading in the meanings and scenarios prevailing in our social system, or of learning to interpret the Bible in terms of scenarios appropriate to social systems familiar to biblical authors. That, of course, entails learning about other social systems and their structures and values, which might radically differ from our own.

ANTHROPOLOGY AND INTERPRETATION

Because biblical documents come from historical periods and social systems so different from our own, in reading and studying the Bible, the reader/scholar is fundamentally an eavesdropper. The persons described in biblical documents are fundamentally foreigners. Therefore, the modern reader must ask: How might one develop a comparative perspective to facilitate understanding? What sort of information is lacking and what sort of information is needed to allow for adequate interpretation? This is where cultural anthropology fits into the biblical interpreter's repertory. By "cultural anthropology" I mean that social science that studies human societies and their social systems in a comparative way. Cultural anthropology is essentially concerned with the cross-cultural, comparative understanding of persons in foreign or alien social groups, specifically in terms of how they differ from us and from our social group(s). Such study looks to comparative differences in the way human beings learn to interpret the objects in their environment. These objects notably comprise the major bearers of human meaning: self, others, nature, time, space, and the All. Along with interpretations based on and derived from comparison, anthropologists are equally interested in structures or patterns of behavior that human groups create and utilize in order to realize and express the meanings and feelings that are invested in self, others, nature, time, space, and the All. Such structures are called social institutions.

Cultural anthropology, with its emphasis on comparison, would require that one begin by acquiring adequate, reflexive knowledge about the structures, functions, values, and meanings of one's own society (usually studied by sociologists and social psychologists) as well as adequate information about the social dimensions of human living in those areas of concern. In our case, these are the areas from which the documents derive. In the discussion that follows, I shall be concerned exclusively with the New Testament, a corpus of writings that comes from the eastern Mediterranean in the Greco-Roman Period. What are the traditional values of the Mediterranean? What are traditional Mediterranean social structures: kinship, polity, economics, religion, education? What are the traditional meanings and values attached to self (male and female), others (our group, their group), nature (domestic and wild), time (linear or cyclical), space (inside, outside, male and female), the All (images of God, gods)? Perhaps the first step in acquiring such information is to learn about the present-day values and social structures of the Mediterranean (for example, Boissevain 1979; Davis 1977; Gilmore 1982; Peristiany 1965; Pitt-Rivers 1968b).

It is necessary to exercise one's imagination with some appropriate set of data. History derives from socially tutored imagination. While historians are masters at gathering data sets, they rarely explain what configuration of data is appropriate to retroject into some ancient social system. While history must be imaginative, it should not be imaginary. What sort of filters must one employ to keep out the imaginary, to avoid anachronism and ethnocentrism? I use comparative social-scientific models and constructs to help in the imaginative process as well as to avoid the imaginary. Obviously, information about present-day eastern Mediterraneans cannot be imported wholesale into the scenarios of New Testament times without the help of some historical filters (see Cohn 1980; Elliott 1994b). Yet comparative information about traditional, present-day Mediterranean social groups helps to set the dimensions of possible, and even probable, scenarios. They describe approximate examples and instances, and may serve as a negative control for current interpretation. Thus, if traditional, present-day Mediterranean groups view the world largely in terms of a sexual division of labor rooted in conceptions of honor and shame, and historical research attests to the presence of this scenario from time immemorial in the region (for example, Homer, Old Testament, Greco-Roman world; see Pitt-Rivers 1977; Davis 1984), chances are high that this peculiar form of social organization was present in New Testament times as well (overwhelmingly demonstrated by Neyrey 1998). To replace the first-century Mediterranean view of the world with some post-Enlightenment, Industrial Revolution model of individualism applied to nonelite persons results in an anachronistic reading of the New Testament (for example, as recently done by Schüssler Fiorenza 1983; John Miller 1997; see Malina 1996b; Pilch 1997). If people in a post-Enlightenment, industrial society seek to understand first-century Mediterranean peasant society in its gender-separate, nonindividualistic terms, they would do well not to look to their own societies nor to societies far afield (such as India or Iran or Malaya), but rather to consider the latest expressions of traditional Mediterranean society. The negative control such values and structures provide indicates that some interpretations cannot be correct. For example, if Mediterranean persons are still enculturated into such aspects of corporate personality as honor and shame, factionalism, and challenge-riposte, with gender-based values loaded upon self, others, nature, time, space, and the All, there would be high probability that these features are to be found in the New Testament. Therefore, interpretations that do not find these aspects of the corporate personality or that omit them must necessarily be wrong, or at least inadequate. By the same token, to omit, eliminate, or overlook these cultural data and assumptions in one's reading of the New Testament requires that they be replaced by something else. Post-Enlightenment individualism, romantic love, modern views of friendship between the sexes, and a guilt and achievement orientation based on efficiency simply cannot be present in the New Testament texts, because there is no evidence of these phenomena in present or past Mediterranean peasant peoples.

My presupposition is the medieval logical insight: to proceed deductively from the possible to the actual is invalid. Just because something is possible does not mean it actually exists or existed. On the other hand, to proceed from what exists to what might have existed is logically valid. If something exists today that appears to be identical with something ancient, chances are high that they share similar function and meaning. One can then approximate contemporary meanings to ancient situations within the same category—all things being equal (*A posse ad esse non valet illatio; ab esse ad posse valet illatio*). A question Bible readers usually ask is: Is it possible that people actually spoke and behaved in the way I am led to imagine on the basis of the experience I bring to my reading of the gospels? The answer, of course, is yes. All "Is it possible . . ." questions mean "Can you, too, imagine what I can?" But the more significant question is: Are there any people on the planet today who speak and behave in the way we are told people did in the first-century world? If people actually speak and behave similarly to first-century people, we can come to an understanding of the past by building a comparative model to weed out historical accretions, ethnocentric appropriations, and other low context errors and come up with something that better approximates the social system of the time and place described in the New Testament.

The thought of using contemporary behavior to retroject into the past after being duly filtered makes proper historians break out in a mental rash that reveals their allergies to social-scientific perspectives (see, for example, Judge 1980). Historians prefer inductive evidence demonstrating the existence of any ancient behavioral pattern. To postulate them would be faulty method. Yet such proper historians rarely reveal the implicit models that they postulate and employ for collecting what they believe to be evidence, and then for interpreting the presumed evidence thus collected. I call this approach the "immaculate perception" approach. Richard Horsley articulates this viewpoint very well in his rather incomprehensible critique of social-scientific criticism. He seems to think that the purpose behind employing social science models is to illustrate the models, not to generate understanding of ancient documents and the behavior described in those documents.

> Such studies illustrating social science models from New Testament texts involve a questionable presumption of continuity (in effect) from findings of modern anthropologists to the realities of ancient Hellenistic Roman life. . . . If in the absence of literary or other evidence, we are to give credence to presumptions of historical continuity, then for the Palestinian peasantry among whom the Synoptic Gospel traditions originated it would make far more sense to imagine continuity with the role and values we know through biblical literature and history in the preceding centuries. Such continuity, moreover, would appear to be confirmed by the values manifested in ancient popular movements more contemporary with Jesus known through Josephus and other ancient writers. (Horsley 1994: 14, n. 22)

The fact is that, without some interpretative matrix, one cannot "know" the "roles and values we know through biblical literature and history in the preceding centuries." All such knowledge is the outcome of an interpretative enterprise, and historians as a rule rarely tell their audiences how they came up what they consider evidence and how they developed the story they tell. As far as I know, social-scientific interpretations of the New Testament have always proceeded by critically and hypothetically adapting and revising social-scientific models adequate to the task of reading ancient Mediterranean documents, then studying those sources while refashioning the models on the basis of information provided by ancient documents and archaeological artifact. The process—reasoning from hypothesis to data and back again as much as necessary to gain an insight—is called "abduction" by the philosopher Charles Peirce (Malina 1991b). It is the ordinary process used in scientific study, whether in the natural sciences or in the humanities. It describes how humans understand.

Aside from fundamentalistic belief in immaculate perception, modern Bible readers, nonprofessional and professional, continually import anachronistic perspectives, values, and attitudes into the documents they study. In assessing persons and events, first-century Mediterraneans made do without a number of "obvious" presuppositions that are now quite common among readers of ancient texts. First-century Mediterraneans were ethnically particularistic to the extent that each ethnic group was a species distinct from other ethnics—as distinct as lion and dog. Aside from Roman views of the *oikoumene* as their world, first-century Mediterraneans had no universalistic political pretensions. There were no nation states, only ethnic groups and their territories. Roman statesmen dealt with other ethnic groups in terms of good faith based on patterns of clientelism. Roman elites believed that their political control of the Mediterranean basin was like that of a patron, not a domineering autocratic imperial tyrant. Roman elites wanted subject peoples to behave like clients. To behave otherwise was to be a rebel, an outlaw. No one in the first century believed all human beings could be endowed with equal rights. Men, like their gods, were tied to locales and to their ingroup. Since Mediterraneans believed that people existed in various species, allegiances always followed ingroup/outgroup patterns. Ethnic groups, males and females, slaves and free, aristocrats and plebeian, formed various species according to the dispositions of nature. Individuals are best known by the nonpsychological, stereotypical qualities of their groups and essentially represented their groups. The notion of the individual as a unique, idiosyncratic universe came rather late in European history (see Mesnil 1981: 203–34 and especially Duby and Braunstein 1988: 507–630). And while the ability to think with empathy—in the sense of political impartiality—was evidenced, for example, by Thucydides, this is hardly the psychological empathy, much less the "interpathy," commonly available in the West today (see Augsburger 1986: 27–29). There was no sense of history, much less of social criticism. Thus nearly all the modes of perception presently available and in vogue among twentieth-century interpreters enculturated in Euro-American societies simply did not exist in the first-century Mediterranean (see Veyne 1989 passim).

ANCIENT "RELIGION"

But perhaps the most significant obstacle blocking comparative access to the societies of the New Testament period is the widespread belief that Jesus and his program were about religion. It is quite common in the world of biblical scholarship as well as among ancient historians to find such straightforward and anthropologically innocent statements as: "In the ancient world in general, and in Israel in particular, the dominant beliefs and institutions were explicitly religious and were embodied in traditions passed on from generation to generation" (Collins 1983: 2). Similarly: "Religious affirmation was the business of the biblical writers, and the business of many of those whose deeds and words have been recorded by them" (Addinall 1994: 137). Most who research and describe ancient religion rarely tell us what it is they are specifically dealing with. Yet some will sprinkle their work with pop-psychological descriptions of the function of religion. For example, MacMullen (1981: 57) informs us that religion serves to satisfy some common emotional wants. Religion is what "actually stimulates its inhabitants to significantly different levels of emotion in the service of their god or gods" (ibid.: 65). He even finds modern popular sociology in antiquity: "It was certainly recognized throughout antiquity . . . that religion served to strengthen the existing social order" (ibid.). In summary, the topic of religion is presumed to be self-evident to first-century peoples, as it is to the modern reader. And the social settings and functions of religion are equally presumed to have been much as they are today.

In turn, sociologists of religion and social anthropologists in their wake have been in search of generalizable principles for a model of religion that might fit all societies, past and present (see Morris 1987). They have given considerable attention to ancient societies to supplement the limited data concerning the religious life of unadulterated contemporary primitive religious systems. In the attempt to avoid anachronism and ethnocentrism, a number of biblical scholars have turned to the sociology of religion to provide models for the understanding of religion in New Testament times (for example, to Wilson 1975). But since the sociology of religion derives from the study of contemporary religion, it would seem that the best the sociology of religion can do and has done for biblical scholars is to tell us what New Testament people would be like if they lived today (for example, Stark 1996).

The situation is quite comparable in the field of economics. Those concerned with comparative economics and economic anthropology witness to a schism based on a methodological dispute labeled the substantivist-formalist (or primitivist-modernist) controversy. Substantivists believe economic systems of the past cannot be understood in terms of modern systems at all. Peasant and other preindustrial economic systems were always embedded in kinship and/or politics (see especially Polanyi 1968). So while all human societies have an economic institution to provision society, this social institution was not the free-standing, separate object of concern that it has become for us, notably after the eighteenth century (the Enlightenment; U.S. as Enlightenment experiment; and Adam Smith's *The Wealth of Nations*, 1776). The economic institution existed substantively, as domestic economy or as political economy, but not as "the economy." Formalists would argue that even though this was the case, nevertheless, modern principles and models of the economy fit all societies of all times, in their own way (see Lowry 1979; Dalton 1961). This debate and its models are quite parallel and relevant to the study of religion. A separation of church and state, of religion and politics, was inconceivable until the same period (and in terms of the same ideology) as the split of economics from politics and kinship. For it was the Enlightenment, and the United States as Enlightenment experiment, that proposed the dislodging of established religion from politics. If this were indeed a novel step, what was society like before the great separation? Obviously religion was embedded in politics and kinship, as was economics.

However, the fact that the separation of church and state is an eighteenth-century occurrence, the fact that the separation of bank/market and state was first articulated by Adam Smith in 1776, and that the first Enlightenment government requiring separation of denominational religion and state is an equally eighteenth-century phenomenon, should at least lead ancient historians to pause before generalizing on the basis of contemporary Euro-American experience. The facts indicate that before these eighteenth-century Enlightenment transformations, church and state as well as bank/market and state were quite fused. In sum, the task of New Testament interpretation entails reading sources with the use of comparative scenarios culled from the first-century Mediterranean world and the interpreter's contemporary world (Malina 1991a). If cultural anthropology is the comparative study of the meanings various human groups develop to live in a socially meaningful, human way, the task of New Testament interpretation will always have an anthropological component, explicit or implicit. The sets of meanings typical of a given social group form the social scenarios that people in the group carry around in their heads and/or hearts. And it is in terms of such scenarios that people interpret their experience and those of others. To understand any sort of communication, both sender and receiver of the message must share some social scenario; otherwise, the result is noise or putting words into the mouth of the sender; in other words, the result is a distorted message. If we share nothing of the social scenarios that shaped the perspectives of the biblical authors, our Bible reading and subsequent theologizing will be either noise or our own ideas and values imposed on those authors and their texts.

What, then, is the kingdom of God about? To what sort of social situation was it meant to be a solution? The chapters that follow set out a range of models that should assist the considerate, contemporary reader of the New Testament to better understand Jesus' proclamation to his contemporaries.

Statue of the Roman emperor Tiberius, Pergamon Museum, Berlin

ಌ 1 ಌ

WHY PROCLAIM THE
KINGDOM OF GOD?

Before the significant eighteenth-century Enlightenment transformations that set so many of the major ground rules of contemporary living, church and state as well as bank/market and state were consolidated. In the political sphere, along with governmental institutions there were political religion, and political economy, but no separate religion and economy. And what about the matrix of the political, namely kinship? While families were structured in terms of prevailing kinship patterns, here, too, were domestic economy and domestic religion but no separate religion and economy (see Malina 1986a; 1994a). While we generally attend to kinship, politics, religion, and economics (among other institutions), only kinship and politics were of explicit focal concern to the ancients.

This kind of societal perspective is crucial to understanding biblical documents, because it is a truism that meanings derive from social systems. Without knowledge of the social system of first-century Mediterraneans writing in Greek or Hebrew, modern students can only presume they are hearing or reading English in Greek or Hebrew wording. The same is true, of course, of the many American high school students who can speak English in Spanish, German, and French. Just as understanding social systems is crucial to learning the meanings of foreign languages, it is fundamental to cross-cultural communication. And studying the New Testament historically is at bottom an exercise in cross-cultural understanding in a historical register. If meaning in language and other forms of behavior derive from social systems, what in fact are social systems?

Social Systems

Social systems consist of social institutions, value sets, and person types. From the viewpoint of our own experience, all societies might be viewed as consisting of (at least) four major social institutions: kinship, politics, economics, and religion (after Parsons 1960). Social institutions are fixed forms of phases of social life. They do not exist independently of each other, except in terms of the modes of perception and interpretation into which members of a group are socialized. Institutions are the ways or means that people use to realize meaningful, human social living within a given society. Briefly, *kinship* is about naturing and nurturing people; it is held together by commitment (also called loyalty or solidarity) and forms a structure of human belonging. *Economics* is about provisioning a group of people; it is held together by inducement, that is, the exchange of goods and services, and forms the adaptive structure of a society. *Politics* looks to effective collective action; it is held together by power and forms the vertical organizational structure of a society. Finally, *religion* deals with the overarching order of existence, with meaning; it is held together by influence; it provides reasons for what exists and the models that generate those reasons. Therefore, religion forms the meaning system of a society and, as such, feeds back and forward into the kinship, economic, and political systems, unifying the whole by means of some explicit or implicit ideology (see Table 1, below).

Since the documents contained in the Bible surely antedate the Enlightenment, the authors of those documents simply did not deal with religion or economics as areas of consideration separable from kinship and politics. Instead, kinship and political norms determined how economic and religious perceptions and behaviors were conceived and articulated. In other words, the authors of biblical documents were enculturated in societies in which the social institutions of kinship and politics were the exclusive arenas of life. Biblical documents come from a world of domestic religion and political religion, as well as domestic economy and political economy. Biblical authors never spoke of economics purely and simply; their language was not used to express systems of meaning derived from a complex and technologically oriented society. This was not because their language could not be used to speak of economics and religion, of technology and science. Modern Hebrew and Greek speakers do speak of these matters. Rather, the reason for this absence is, by all evidence, that the social systems of the period simply did not focus on freestanding economic and religious institutional concerns. Technology was boring and low-status, best left to anonymous manual workers and slaves. Consequently, the vocabulary and system of distinctions of the various ideologies expressed in the Bible worked within kinship and politics. Conceptions of the henotheistic "God of Israel" are expressed in kinship and political terms. The language of covenant and law was and is derivative of politics, just as the language of worship and ritual was and is derivative of kinship and political forms of behavior. There is no developed biblical terminology descriptive of the pragmatics of adaptation (economics) and the abstract meanings rooted in it. Hence, biblical documents reveal a vocabulary and syntax employed to realize a range of meanings expressing belonging (the dimension rooted in kinship) and power (the dimension rooted in politics), but almost nothing to express reasoned influence (the dimension rooted in the meaning of religious institution) and inducement (the dimension rooted in economics). Rather, influence (religion) is made to work through belonging and power—not on its own terms, since these terms are always inflated (wild assertions and exaggerations). Moreover, inducement (economics) has to be converted through and into belonging (for example, wealth is meaningless unless convertible into honor), and thus has no focus in and of itself. This lack of economic focus is replicated in the prohibition of interest for loans (for example, Deut 23:19-20). Similarly, in the Hellenistic and Roman periods, this lack of focus reveals itself in disdain for the status and role of merchant and for acquired wealth (see Malina 1993: 103–7). Plutarch, for example, notes that merchants are simply not necessary in a society. He tells of Lycurgus who "brought about the banishment from Sparta of everything not absolutely necessary. And, by reason of this, no merchant, no public lecturer, no soothsayer or mendicant priest, no maker of fancy articles ever made his way into Sparta" (*Sayings of Spartans* 226D; LCL).

We might sketch the four major social institutions in the form of a baseball diamond, with kinship at home plate and politics at second base. Economics would be at first base and religion at third base. The picture would be like the model on the following page (Table 1). The rules of the game of life on a field consisting of these four social institutions serving as bases on a baseball field would have to change radically if we got rid of first and third. And this was the case in antiquity. Only two social institutions were focal: kinship and politics. Without the other two explicit bases, the field now consists of home and second—a ball game with two points of movement, just like cricket and its two wickets. The point of this example is that living in the first-century Mediterranean differs from post-Enlightenment social arrangements as much as cricket differs from baseball: two entirely different games with entirely different rules replicating entirely different cultural systems. On the other hand, what they have in common is that they are human social systems enabling meaningful, human, social ways of living. Humans can be enculturated in and live according to either form—but not at the same time.

Legend: Social Institution
          (Societal Subsystem)
          Mediating Symbol

TABLE 1
Four Basic Institutions of Human Society
(for more information see Malina 1986a; 1986b)

Meanings shared by first-century people situated around the northeast littoral of the Mediterranean were encoded in patterns of language and behavior deriving from various but similar social systems constituting the Roman Empire. From our point of view, what is distinctive about life in the Roman Empire is that living took place in two somewhat overlapping arenas called kinship and politics. Kinship was the focal and overwhelmingly significant social institution, of greatest concern to the collectivistic individuals who formed societies at the time. It was largely elite kinship groups ("the best families") that played in the arena called politics. Even with broad local variation, daily life in this period was daily life in the Roman Empire (see Hacquard 1952; Dupont 1992). In other words, while Greek, Roman, and Semitic kinship forms differed, kinship was fundamental to each group. And while democracy, monarchy, aristocracy, and theocracy differed from each other, all were political institutions whose roles and statuses fell to the best families. All kinship forms had their domestic religion and domestic economy; all political forms had their political religion and political economy. Because of these similarities noticeable at a higher level of abstraction, the various peoples of the region could understand each other. And it is such institutional configurations that make them so entirely different from us.

RURALIZED SOCIETY

Another distinctive feature common to the Mediterranean region in the first century was that the whole Roman *oikoumene* had a similar societal thrust, best characterized as a ruralized society (Southall 1998 also uses this designation). What I mean by ruralized society is that great landowners set the agenda for the empire on the basis of their interests, values, and concerns. This point should become clearer from the following considerations. It is a truism among urban historians that, at present, the United States is an urbanized society (Hays 1993). Urban areas contain most of the national population and urban agendas determine national policies. Urban concerns dominate the goals, values, and behaviors of the 5 percent of the population that is engaged in agricultural production.

Our urbanized society is quickly developing into one with a global outreach. The United States became an urban society over the period marked by the rise of industrialization to the end of the Second World War. An urban society, in this perspective, is one in which a significant proportion of the population lives and works in urban centers, following an agenda quite different from rural society yet in somewhat tandem rhythms. In urban societies, urban agendas compete with rural ones in determining national policies. Urban and rural agendas foster conflicting goals, values, and behaviors. Before the waves of immigration at the end of the nineteenth century and the first quarter of the twentieth, the United States was essentially a rural society, with rural agendas determining national policies and rural concerns dominating the goals, values, and behaviors of the 95 percent of the population living on the land and the 5 percent living permanently in cities (for features of each type of society, see Table 2, taken from Malina 2000). While the Roman *oikoumene* had 98 percent or more of its populations living on the land, Roman imperial society differed essentially from eighteenth- and

TABLE 2
Types of Society

RURALIZED SOCIETY	RURAL SOCIETY 2: URBAN DEPOT SOCIETY	URBAN INDUSTRIAL SOCIETY	URBANIZED SOCIETY
• Ancient *polis/civitas*	• Medieval city, city before Industrial Revolution	• Industrial Revolution city	• Agglomerative urban areas
City Type	*City Type*	*City Type*	*City Type*
• Administrative central places	• Depot cities	• Industrial cities	• Informational cities
City Focus	*City Focus*	*City Focus*	*City Focus*
• Bundle of consumption demands and pressures locally satisfied from subsistence by force	• Bundle of consumption demands and pressures satisfied from surplus by reciprocity	• Bundle of consumption demands and pressures stimulated by technology needs	• Bundle of consumption demands and pressures stimulated by marketing agents
• Necessities	• Necessities • City conveniences	• Necessities • City conveniences • Personal conveniences	• Necessities • City conveniences • Personal conveniences • Amenities
• Food, clothing, shelter	• Food, clothing, shelter • City technology	• Food, clothing, shelter • City technology • Personal technology	• Food, clothing, shelter • City technology • Personal technology • Information
Roads	*Roads*	*Roads*	*Roads*
• Local patterns to central place	• Intercity patterns	• Industrial interregional patterns	• Global patterns
Source of Technology	*Source of Technology*	*Source of Technology*	*Source of Technology*
• Rural origin	• Rural origin	• City: mechanic	• City: electronic
Meaning of Open Places	*Meaning of Open Places*	*Meaning of Open Places*	*Meaning of Open Places*
• Wilderness and desert, to be avoided	• Wilderness and desert, to be avoided	• Industrial waste disposal	• Lands, rivers, air, oceans, and ground water—off limits to waste disposal

(Table 2 continued on next page)

RURALIZED SOCIETY	RURAL SOCIETY 2: URBAN DEPOT SOCIETY	URBAN INDUSTRIAL SOCIETY	URBANIZED SOCIETY
Citizens	*Citizens*	*Citizens*	*Citizens*
• Land-holding city elites or those of value to city elites	• City residents	• Nationals Type I	• Nationals Type II
Elites	*Elites*	*Elites*	*Elites*
• Agriculturalists	• Merchants	• Urban industrialists and bankers	• Urban information managers
Labor Force	*Labor Force*	*Labor Force*	*Labor Force*
• Agricultural	• Mercantile	• Industrial	• Informational
Scope of Communication	*Scope of Communication*	*Scope of Communication*	*Scope of Communication*
• Local	• Interurban	• Regional	• Global
Empire Control	*Empire Control*	*Empire Control*	*Empire Control*
• Elite agriculturalists control empire	• Elite merchants control empire	• Elite urbanites control national empire	• Elite urbanites control multinational empire
Surplus Control	*Surplus Control*	*Surplus Control*	*Surplus Control*
• Created by force	• By pact	• By monopoly	• By market
Agriculture Control	*Agriculture Control*	*Agriculture Control*	*Agriculture Control*
• Owner/producers	• Warehousers	• Processors	• Marketers
• Crops determined by owners/growers (staples)	• Crops determined by growers and elite demands (staples)	• Crops determined by processors and market demands	• Crops determined by marketers and created market demands
• Inalienable land considered alienable; all taken region without central place was "desert"	• Alienable land; feudal and communal ownership	• Alienable land; abandoned land becomes public land	• Alienable land, private and public ownership
Residence	*Residence*	*Residence*	*Residence*
• Elites have country estates and city houses	• Elites live in city or in country houses	• Elites have city or country houses	• Nonelites have city or country houses
Nature	*Nature*	*Nature*	*Nature*
• Source of commodities; extractive farm and forest elite economy; wild nature to be destroyed and controlled	• Source of commodities; extractive farm and forest elite economy; wild nature to be destroyed and controlled	• Source of commodities; extractive farm and forest industrialists but nature to be controlled and preserved for industry	• To be maintained in a pristine state for its own sake •Nature is urbanized; preservation of wilderness

(Table 2 continued on next page)

RURALIZED SOCIETY	RURAL SOCIETY 2: URBAN DEPOT SOCIETY	URBAN INDUSTRIAL SOCIETY	URBANIZED SOCIETY
• Rivers are uncontrollable	• Rivers are uncontrollable; to be used for transport	• Rivers are to be tamed for industrial use	• Rivers are to be left in or returned to natural state
• Wilderness, like desert, is to be feared	• Wilderness to be avoided	• Wilderness to be tamed for industrial use	• Wilderness to be appreciated and enjoyed
• Consumptive view of wildlife	• Consumptive view of wildlife	• Consumptive view of wildlife as industrial value	• Appreciative view of wildlife: to be enjoyed, studied, observed
City Residents	*City Residents*	*City Residents*	*7City Residents*
• City people are rural people, living within their collective resources; subsistence society.	• City people no longer rural people; living off new abundance	• City people were never rural people; living off new national superabundance	• City people are never rural people; now living off national and global resources

nineteenth-century United States rural society in that a mathematically minute minority of extremely large landowners set the agenda for the empire and all its peoples on the basis of their interests, values, and concerns. This was ruralized society.

KINSHIP

Such ruralized societies had their two focal social institutions realized in the spatial and architectural arrangements called the house and the city. The house replicated kinship; the city replicated politics. Kinship is the symboling of biological processes of human reproduction and growth in terms of abiding relations, roles, statuses, and so on. Kinship is about naturing and nurturing human beings interpreted as family members (and neighbors in nonmobile societies; admittedly, specific kinship systems are notoriously difficult to describe and define in detail; for attempts at definition, see Verdon 1981 and notably Keen 1985; for the Roman world see Saller 1984, Hanson 1989a, 1989b, 1990, 1994; Moxnes 1997. The same is true of the fictive or pseudo-kinship relations that express and constitute belonging, solidarity, or loyalty, see Pitt-Rivers

1968a). In ruralized societies, the kinship group was the economic and religious unit as well: the ancient Mediterranean knew domestic economy and domestic religion (but at the family level, no economy or religion separate from kinship).

Domestic religion, for example, used the roles, values, and goals of the household in the articulation and expression of religion. Religious functionaries of domestic religion were household personages (notably fathers and, inside the household, mothers as well, oldest sons, ancestors). Focus was on the deity(ies) as the source of solidarity, mutual commitment, and belonging mediated through ancestors, expected to provide well-being, health, and prosperity for the kin-group and its patriarchs to the benefit of family members. The house had its altars and sacred rites (focused on the family meal and the hearth as symbols of life) with father (patriarch) and mother (first in charge at home) officiating. Deities were tribal and/or household ones (for example, *lares*; *penates*; the God of Abraham, Isaac, Jacob) as well as ancestors who saw to the well-being, prosperity, and fertility of family members. There was much concern about inheritance and the legitimacy of heirs. Domestic religion sought meaning through belonging: an ultimately meaningful existence derives from belonging, for example, to a chosen, select, holy people. In well-ordered societies of the region, it was belonging within the proper ranking in one's well-ordered society (often called hierarchy). In societies in some disarray, it was belonging to a proper kin and/or fictive kin-group (see Malina 1986b; 1994a; 1996a).

In the domestic economy, kinship concerns for naturing and nurturing were replicated in the production and sustenance of new life in agricultural pursuits, a family affair for nonelites. The ingroup/outgroup pattern marking kinship boundaries served as markers between families as well as between the kin-group's political unit and the rest of the world.

POLITICS

The second, equally focal institution in this period was politics—the symboling of social relations in terms of vertical roles, statuses, and interactions. Politics was about effective collective action, the application of force to attain collective goals. The roles, statuses, entitlements, and obligations of the political system were available only to properly pedigreed persons from the best families; they were tied to the kinship system. The political unit was likewise an economic and religious one:

ancient Mediterraneans knew political economy and political religion (at the political level, there was no economy or religion separate from politics). Political concerns for effective collective action on behalf of the ingroup were replicated in the application of force on outgroups, largely in the interest of elite domestic economic concerns: acquisition of more land, labor, animals, and so on.

Political religion, in turn, employed the roles, values, and goals of politics in the articulation and expression of religion: religious functionaries were political personages; focus was on the deity(ies) as the source of power and might, expected to provide order, well-being, and prosperity for the body politic and its power wielders (elites) to the benefit of subjects. In monarchic city-territories of the eastern Mediterranean, temples were political buildings, and temple sacrifices were for the public good; the deity of the temple had a staff similar to the one a monarch had in the palace (majordomo = high priest; officials of various ranks and grades = priests, levites; temple slaves, etc.; see Elliott 1991). "Democratic" cities controlled by local elites altered monarchic temples into democratic ones, now owned and run by city councils or noble council members, with sacrifice offered according to the wishes of the sacrificing entity.

CITY AND COUNTRY

The great landowners shaped the agenda of daily life for society at large. These great landowners, the best people (or aristocrats), generally had two residences. One was a house in the countryside, on the land that provided these elite persons with power and wealth. The other was a house built as part of a cluster of such houses of other landowning elites in a central (or nodal) place, the city (see Rohrbaugh 1991; Oakman 1991). Just as small holders lived in houses clustered together (usually for support and protection) in towns and villages, so did the large holders, but their housing clusters formed the center of what the ancients called a *polis* (Gr.), *urbs* or *civitas* (Lat.), or *'ir* (Heb.).

The ancient city, in fact, was a bounded, centralized set of selective kinship relationships concerned with effective collective action and expressed spatially in terms of architecture and the arrangement of places. The centralized set of social relationships among elites took on spatial dimension by means of territoriality; that is, these elites claimed dominance of their central place and its surround. This is simply one dimension of the effective collective action that defines a political institution. Large numbers of people were required to support the elites and their concerns both in the country and in the city. Resident city support consisted of retainers that constituted the nonelite central place population.

In other words, the first-century Mediterranean *civitas* or *polis* was really a large, ruralized central place in which properly pedigreed farmers/ranchers displayed and employed their unbelievable wealth in competitions for honor among each other. Largeholders thus found it in their interest to live periodically near other largeholders in central places that likewise provided them with organized force (an army) to protect their interests from the masses. The elite united to promote and defend their collective honor in face of the outgroup in annual rites of war which, if carried off successfully, brought them more land and/or the produce of that land. They equally participated in the continual, if seasonal, activity of extortion called taxation. Their honor rating, rooted in kinship, brought them the power that brought them further wealth.

Yet for elites, the city house was a secondary dwelling. It was not a private place like the dwellings of the city nonelite. The elite city house was multifunctional, a place of constant socializing, economic, and sometimes political intercourse, and not simply a place of habitation. For these elites, living together essentially served the purpose of daily challenge-riposte interaction in the pursuit of honor.

The primary elite residence was the elite country estate, a place of residence and subsistence (family plus land and buildings for production, distribution, transmission, reproduction, group identification). Nonelite farmers and tenants imagined their limited holdings in terms of the ideal, the elite country estate. Elite country houses were spacious, centrally heated, with a swimming bath, library, works of art, and other luxuries. They were situated on vast agricultural estates worked by slaves in the West, and largely by tenants in the East. "At one time in the first century A.D. fully half of what is today Tunisia belonged to a mere six owners. In France archaeologists have uncovered an estate that embraces twenty-five hundred acres; the farm buildings alone covered forty-five" (Casson 27; for Palestine, see Fiensy 1991; and Hanson and Oakman 1998: 116–19).

The eastern Mediterranean formed the outer reaches of roads that led to Rome. As is well known, Rome was a city that expanded its political web to include most other cities in the Mediterranean basin. Empire (*imperium*) and City (*urbs*) blended into a single entity, with the City at its social geographical center of the inhabited, civilized, world. A number of traditional features typical of ruralized society punctuated life in the city: physical violence, a sense of no control and little responsibility, endless challenges to honor with public humiliation (see Black-Michaud 1975; Boehm 1984). "Roman society demanded an uncomfortable mixture of pervasive deference to superiors and openly aggressive brutishness to inferiors, not just slaves. It was a world of deference and condescension, of curt commands and pervasive threats" (Hopkins 1998: 210–11; see also MacMullen 1974).

THE SIGNIFICANCE OF THE CITY

The Roman Empire was a network of cities rooted in the city of Rome. If our modern cities produce industrial products and information technology, then cities in antiquity essentially produced power sanctioned by force. What Rome attained was a monopoly on power sanctioned by force over the whole *oikoumene*, while local cities were equally devoted to forging the same product, power over those in their surround.

Power personified in the emperor or a god, reified in the central imperial city and its institutions, held full attention. If some deity resident in the sky or manifest on earth was worth its godhead, it had to be omnipotent. It is no accident that Constantine's political religion believed "in one God, the Father, the Almighty . . ." (Nicene Creed, 325 C.E.). The traditional cult of omnipotence can ostensibly trace its roots to the rise of the first central places serving as administrative and residential centers for elites who controlled the agrarian surround. In simpler terms, omnipotence was the focal value of cities from their very inception (see Routledge 1997, and the typology in Rupp 1997). And with overarching value tied to omnipotence, cruelty seems to have been a necessary concomitant—albeit reserved for lower statuses and outgroups, human and nonhuman.

Modern scholars suggest that cruelty is a process of maiming the ordinary patterns of behavior that are some living creature's way of living. Such maiming may affect biological or social ways of living. Maiming makes resistance ineffectual and thus renders the victim passive. For the victimizer, what counts is power over the victim's whole life, even if exercised on a whim, with little concern (Hallie 1982: 26 and passim; see Auguet 1972). And what Romans despised and gloated over, as others have demonstrated, was passivity, especially in males (Veyne 1998). But how is it humanly possible to display such devotion to public displays of physical cruelty as those in the amphitheater and other venues of Roman punishment? Eric Brenman suggests that "in order that cruelty can remain unmodified various mechanisms are employed. The most important processes include the worship of omnipotence, which is felt to be superior to human love and forgiveness, the clinging to omnipotence as a defense against depression, and the sanctification of grievance and revenge. In order to avoid conscious guilt, the perceptions of the mind are narrowed to give ostensible justification to the cruelty, and the obviation of redeeming features in the object" (Brenman 1985: 280; note how these characteristics fit Israeli cruelty to Palestinians or Serbian cruelty to Kosovars).

Perhaps the closest modern experience of living in a first-century eastern Mediterranean city is living in a noncapital city in a developing country (see, for example, Breese 1966; Gugler 1996). For, like the first-century Mediterranean, developing countries, apart from capital cities, form ruralized societies. The elite residents in these cities are large landowners, clustered together for mutual interaction and protection. The vast majority of people live on the land as peasants; elites with their retainers constitute perhaps less than 10 percent of the population. And physical violence is the main way to get things done (for example, El Salvador, Guatemala, Santo Domingo, etc.; see Horsley 1988: 127–43).

Thanks to their city, in the first century the Roman elite formed a power syndicate with a network reaching out to elites in other cities of the region. These elites held a near monopoly on physical force applied in organized fashion, the underpinning of the power that was Rome. The outstanding symbol of Roman power was the Coliseum, replicated in the amphitheaters that characterized Roman colonies and Romanized cities of the empire (Hopkins 1983: 1–30; 201–56). The organized slaughter of animate beings—animal and human—in the games properly announced to the outgroup what Roman policies were about. Rome, in effect, sought to monopolize all power in the circum-Mediterranean.

In the imperial system the essential application of power was to benefit elites and their retainers by the further acquisition of land and its products—vegetable, animal, and human. The essential manifestation of this power was in the periodic extortion exacted for Roman protection in a taxation system for the benefit of elites. How might one imagine social interaction that constituted the macrosystem called the Roman Empire? Consider the following organizational characteristics (see

Taylor 1961). Are they features found in Roman elites that controlled and benefited from the empire?

1. An ongoing interaction by a group of individuals over time (elite interaction in various social settings, such as the Senate, the courts, and business; and intermarriage assured such ongoing interaction).

2. An interaction with fixed patterns of behavior, with distinctive roles, statuses, and specializations (society was hierarchical, with standing coming from birth, as codified in third century).

3. Patterns of corruption of public officials, their agents, and individuals in privileged positions of trust (for example, bribery, nepotism, favoritism).

4. The use or threat of violence (the Roman army and amphitheater witness to this).

5. A lifetime careerist orientation among the participants (the *cursus honorum* of elites indicates as much).

6. A view of (political) activity as instrumental rather than an end in itself (political activity was to gain something: honor, power, wealth, control, etc.).

7. Goal direction toward the long-term accumulation of capital (land), influence, power, and untaxed wealth (requirements of certain sums of money to maintain standing points to this).

8. Patterns of complex (political) activity involving long-term planning and multiple levels of execution and organization (imperial and senatorial governing procedures).

9. Patterns of operation that are interjurisdictional, often international in scope (the spread of the Roman imperium throughout the *oikoumene* witnesses this).

10. Use of fronts, buffers, and illegitimate associates (for example, in long-distance trading, moneylending, and so on).

11. Active attempts at the insulation of key members (of elite families) from risks of identification, involvement, arrest, and prosecution.

12. Maximization of profits through attempts at forming cartels or securing monopolies of markets, enterprises, and (political) matrices.

According to Lupsha (1986: 33), these are the characteristics of organized crime (see also Walters 1990 for a useful model). In the preceding list I have added the comments in parentheses, replaced the word "criminal" with the bracketed word [political], and "land" for capital. Lupsha further notes (ibid.):

> One hallmark of organized crime, compared with other types of criminal activities is that it not only seeks to exploit market disparities, such as supply-demand inequities caused by government decision, over- or underregulation, but that it cannot exist without active interaction with the political system, its agents and institutions. For organized crime to prosper, it needs close ties to the body politic. Without the protection and risk minimization of the political system, the organized criminal cannot operate. (1986: 33)

The Roman imperial system of power and extortion did not require any such symbiotic relationship with the political system, its agents, and institutions, since it was precisely the political system, its agents, and institutions that constituted the Roman imperial system.

The best analogy for imagining the macrosystem called the Roman Empire is the social institution prevailing in southern Italy for several centuries which is generally labeled "organized crime": the Camorra (Naples), Mafia (Sicily), 'Ndrangheta (Calabria), and the like (see Hess 1986).

Like the Mafia in Sicily, the Roman Empire reached a point of nearly all-embracing societal control in the circum-Mediterranean. Romans had a near monopoly on physical violence and therefore had social control in the region. The Roman elite person was not just one who survived largely or wholly on politically supported extortionary activities, but was an integral part of the social system. Since the imperial bureaucracy had a major hand in the selection and appointment of local political elites and their economic affairs (always legal) and had control over the levers of political power and the political economy, the imperial bureaucracy was not part of a subculture but was part of the dominant culture of the region. Roman social control was based on fear, to be sure, but also was based to a large extent on a very broad consensus.

Roman political control was like a power syndicate founded entirely on fear: its function was to provide protection—occasionally genuine but more usually spurious protection from itself—in return for taxes and services. Roman government produced neither goods nor services for its subjects and milked legal and illegal businesses equally. Because it was based on physical violence, it would have been highly unstable. To assure minimal stability, elites required their soldiers to take an oath. All

Roman soldiers were bound by oath to their general. Local elites (*decuriones*) were equally bound by oath to the Roman emperor. There is evidence that it was customary for new Roman citizens to swear allegiance to the elite personage who served as patron in the process. Italians were enfranchised in 91 B.C.E. by Drusus and took an oath of fealty in Drusus's name that ran as follows:

> I swear by Jupiter Capitolinus and the Vesta of Rome and by Mars, the ancestral god of Rome, and by the Sun, the founder of the race (Sol Indiges), and by Earth, the benefactress of living and growing things, and by the demigods, who are the founders of Rome and the heroes who have contributed to increase her domain that I will hold the friend and enemy of Drusus to be my friend and enemy and that I will not spare possessions or the life of my children or of my parents if it be to Drusus' advantage and to the advantage of those who have taken this oath. If I become a citizen by the law of Drusus I will hold Rome as my country and Drusus as my greatest benefactor, and I will share this oath with as many citizens as I can. And if I swear faithfully, may all good things come to me; if falsely, the reverse."
> (from Diodorus Siculus, quoted by Taylor 1977: 188)

Individual emperors and senators came and went, but the system itself continued with little change through the fourth until the fourteenth centuries with the fall of New Rome (Constantinople) and the rise of the Ottoman Empire (see Walston 1986: 135).

In a well-known distinction meant to capture the thrust of organized crime, Alan Block (1983) spoke of enterprise syndicates and power syndicates. Roughly speaking he defines an enterprise syndicate as an organization that provides a real service like prostitution, gambling, or drugs, and a power syndicate as an organization that, as its name suggests, seeks control without providing any service—namely, extortion rackets. The Roman Empire clearly functioned as both enterprise and power syndicate. As enterprise syndicate it provided real services for elites and their retainers, such as land acquisition, slaves, taxes for elites and ingroup clients. As power syndicate the empire's elites sought merely to control without providing any service to outgroups, that is, to the subject peoples.

STYLE OF NONELITE SURVIVAL: PATRONAGE

In terms of formal economics, until the discovery/invention of the deep plow in northern Europe in the early Middle Ages, all economies of the Roman Empire were subsistence economies. Single producers could produce only as much as needed for subsistence in any given year. The economy had no surplus. Then how was it possible for persons to survive in subsistence economies given the type of control and constant extortion applied by the Roman Empire on nonelite peoples? One basic set of such arrangements is found in the various kinship systems, nuclear families, extended families, and clan organizations. An extension of such arrangements may be found in the fictive kinship relationships present in many peasant societies. Status equals made arrangements to support each other in difficult situations as neighbors or friends. Finally, there are a number of typical peasant social mechanisms that function to equalize poverty by means of rituals of conspicuous consumption, almsgiving, and especially patronage.

The patron-client relationship, or clientele system, involved an interchange of noncomparable goods and services between persons of unequal socioeconomic ranks. An extended patron-client network, or clientele system, is important in two distinct ways: one, in its consequences for the political system in which it concretely manifests itself; and two, as an heuristic device for the understanding of a wide range of political behaviors such as nepotism, personalism, or favoritism; and political structures such as cliques, factions, machines, and patronage groups, or "followings" (see Malina 1988; Moxnes 1991).

At the core of the patron-client relationship lie three basic factors that define and differentiate it from other power relationships that occur between individuals or groups. These are unequal status, reciprocity, and proximity (Powell 1977).

First, the patron-client tie develops between two parties unequal in status, wealth, and influence. Second, the formation and maintenance of the relationship depends on reciprocity in the exchange of goods and services. Such mutual exchanges involve noncomparable goods and services, however. In a typical transaction, the low-status person (client) will receive material goods and services intended to reduce or ameliorate his environmental threats, while the high-status person (patron) receives less tangible rewards, such as personal services, indications of esteem, deference, or loyalty (or in Rome, at one time, services of a directly political nature such as voting). Third, the development and maintenance of a patron-client relationship rests heavily on face-to-face contact between the two parties; the exchanges encompassed in the relationship are somewhat intimate and highly particularistic and depend upon such proximity.

The features of the patron-client pattern stay the same—whether the parties are individuals, which is often the case—or kinship groups, extended kinship groups, informal or formal voluntary groups, or even institutions. Within many agricultural communities the patron status is highly correlated with landownership and the client status with poor cultivators dependent upon the patron's land for their livelihood.

Consider the tenancy arrangements typical of Galilee, Judea, and Perea. During the time of Jesus, largeholdings increased while private smallholdings diminished. Local peasants had to work the land they previously and customarily possessed within the framework of tenancy. Extremely wealthy landowners provide the newly landless with land (and other items, such as tools and seed) to work in return for a specified share of the harvest (and other items, such as labor). This relationship and its obligations, called tenancy, is established by contract, written or unwritten, in conformity with custom and, more unusually, with law. In practice, such institutional arrangements often fall short of what they are intended to realize. Tenants may face emergencies ranging from family illness to drought. They may have to make provisions for the following year yet lack certainty of tenure. The landowner can see to such needs of his tenant, but the landowner is not obliged to do so under the tenancy agreement. Any help afforded beyond the bare bones of the contract is favor (or grace). The tenants, in turn, are under no obligation to show respect, affection, or friendly feelings to the owner of the land they work. Yet in peasant societies, landowners look for respect since what counts to them, as well as to their tenants, is honor; landowners need the status support that only their tenants can give them. "The establishment of special relationship between a landowner and *some* of his tenants, and an assurance of conspicuous deference and loyalty to the landlord, constitutes the patron-client addendum to the institutionalized landlord-tenant relationship" (Landé 1977: xxi).

All patron-client societies have a number of features in common, features we find in the Roman *oikoumene*. To begin with, political and domestic economies involve large areas of land with minimum outlay on the part of owners; the same is true of their extraction activities. Economic management is concerned with plundering rather than developing. Taxation exists for the benefit of elites, not for the common good. Political and domestic economic activity looks to the expansion of control of ever-larger domains or territories rather than looking to internal improvement. Furthermore, there is intensive exploitation of a fixed resource base. There is a low level of specialization with little concern for technology. Finally, trade is oriented outward to elites in other cities. Such trade is regulated by political authorities and often carried out by conscripted external groups (Eisenstadt and Roniger 1984: 208; Carney 1973). Of course these are all features of the Roman Empire and of local democracies and monarchies in the empire.

The system worked well in Italy even in the face of encroaching Roman hegemony. For example, archaeological evidence from Volaterrae in the Caecina Valley of Italy (near Pisa) indicates that the pre-Roman arrangements of land into smallholdings, largeholdings, villas, and so on remained unaltered through Roman encroachment and Roman conquest. How was this possible? Who protected the locals from Roman imperial tentacles? The evidence suggests that local elites allowed themselves (and their resources) to be co-opted by the Romans in return for the status quo in the region. Local elites proved to be most effective patrons on behalf of their local clients, successfully implanting their city and its region into the Roman Empire with little disturbance to life as previously lived. After all, peasants know they will be taxed, and it mattered little whether the taxes went to the local elites or to some distant elites. The successful mediation of Vollaterrae's local elites led to no discernible alteration in life as lived until Roman encroachment and after (see Terrenato 1998).

But what about Palestine? Jesus' proclamation of the kingdom of God points to an entirely different turn of events. Of the recourse peasants might have in their recurrent plight, extended family was out of the question. Rural housing patterns in first-century Palestine reveal space only for nucleated families (Guijarro 1997; 1998: 47–159). Peasants in both Volaterrae and Palestine considered land to be a sacred, inalienable domestic holding. But unlike in Volaterrae, Israelite lands were treated by Israelite elites as a saleable commodity (Hanson and Oakman 1998: 101–6, 116–19). Moreover, the archaeology of Galilee, Judea, and Perea in the period of Roman expansion points to the gradual disappearance of smallholdings and the increased growth of largeholdings. The evidence points to Israelite elites remiss in their obligations to local clients. Instead of mediating with the Romans for a status quo situation, it seems Israel's aristocrats chose to use their own power and the Roman presence to constrain local peasantry beyond endurable limits. Even some largeholders fell before the tactics of Israelite elites. These disappropriated largeholders became the social bandits know to us from Josephus and the gospel stories. If you look for marginalized persons, it would be these disappropriated largeholders, since peasants were integral to the system while such impoverished aristocrats were not. It was these disappropriate largeholders who became the social bandits of the region (see Horsley and Hanson 1985: 48–87; Hanson and Oakman 1998: 86–90).

Consequently, if the coming of a theocracy to Israel was to make sense to Israelites in Galilee, Judea, and Perea, it would have to be presented to a population ready to see theocracy as a solution to local problems. To return to the question with which I began: What was the problem to which the proclamation of the kingdom of God (political religion) was to be a solution? It was the problem posed by Roman political economy as appropriated by local Israelite aristocracy. The poor, the hungry, and the thirsty could look forward to an imminent resolution to their difficulties. Israel's aristocrats failed in their traditional social roles. This meant Israel's political system—including its political economy and political religion—were at fault. For the prophet from Galilee, the advent of the kingdom of God, Israelite theocracy, entailed the God of Israel taking over the country, resulting in a new political system. For peasants in the region, the collapse of Israel's patronage system meant tragedy in the face of recurrent peasant ills such as disease, accident, natural disasters, and early death, as well as mounting social ills due to peasant vulnerability, misfortune, and land deprivation. Thus it is no surprise that in Jesus' proclamation, the role that the God of Israel would play on behalf of his people was not that of monarch but of "Father." In a political register, "father" was a designation for patron in a patronage system (Stevenson 1992 misses the point). The coming of the kingdom of God marked the advent of a patron for all Israel, the Father in the Sky: a topic to which I turn in the final chapter.

In summary, Jesus' career played out in the Roman Empire. In the eastern Mediterranean, Roman power shared by local elites made cruelty and extortion part of daily living. For the nonelite people of Israel, the collapse of elite Israelite patronage appeared as veritable betrayal and disloyalty on the part of the aristocratic best families on whose behalf the political economy and political religion functioned. Rescue from this situation could only occur with the God of Israel taking control of the country and restoring divine patronage in face of the political perfidy that filled the land. Jesus' proclamation of the kingdom of God was, indeed, his social gospel.

Miniature illuminated manuscript painting of the fall of Jerusalem in 70 C.E. from the Rhyming Bible by Jacob van Maerlant, 1332

᭤ 2 ᭤

MEDITERRANEAN
VIOLENCE
AND THE KINGDOM

The previous chapter broached the topic of the violence characteristic of the many societies of the first-century Mediterranean. In this chapter, I consider the qualities of the violence that Jesus had to deal with as depicted in the New Testament writings. It is important to define this topic, since so much is said about violence in New Testament times that is quite mucilaginous. For example, Richard Horsley (1987) has written an interesting volume on Jesus and the spiral of violence, along with other essays on the topic. His attempt to describe and/or define the concept of violence remains unclear and unfocused in its results. One is hard pressed to know what he is talking about, since he applies the term "violence" whenever one person attempts to have an effect on another; in Horsley's view, moving a child from harm's way or throwing a child in front of a car would both be violence. With such gummy notions as "spiritual violence" and such imprecise categories as "psychological violence," one can hardly feel any more enlightened than when one started the book. As a rule, physical force, or simply force, seems to be what Horsley means by violence. The question, then, is whether the spiral of violence he intends to analyze is really nothing more than a spiral of physical force. Who has to hit whom to get hit back, as when young children start a fight? The Romans—like Mediterraneans in general, including Israel—were agonistic (fight-prone), hence willing to engage in physical conflict at the slightest provocation. For majority peoples, this is simply big-bullyism writ large. And this is what Rome was about in the *oikoumene* as well as

what Jerusalemites were about in their own sphere of influence. Furthermore, as Israel's normative story and sacred writings indicate, this
is how the God of Israel intends his people to be as well. He directs his
chosen people "to purge the evil from the midst of you" (Deut 13:5;
17:7; 19:19; 22:21, 24; 24:7), even by making a "holocaust" (a whole
burnt offering) of those of their cities serving other gods (Deut 13:12-
17; Joshua shows how the program of genocide has good biblical
precedence).

To open with a description, violence is about coercing others in a way
that social norms do not endorse. Socially unauthorized coercion
employed with a view to maintaining, defending, or restoring the status
quo is a form of behavior called establishment violence or vigilantism.
The fact that the perpetrators of violence in this instance are persons
devoted to the status quo accounts for the qualifier "establishment." Such
persons prefer things as they are. Not only do they prefer the status
quo—they are quite prepared to vent their vehement antipathies on
those espousing significant change, whether it be creative change or
restorative change. The gospel story clearly reveals that Jesus' death was
the outcome of establishment violence.

The purpose of this chapter is to describe a scenario of establishment
violence that might be adequate for understanding some dimensions of
Jesus' proclamation of the kingdom of God as well for comprehending
the reaction of his opponents.

Establishment Violence
in the New Testament

The story of Jesus is full of instances of persons, visible and invisible,
doing or planning violence toward others in the name of the status quo.
These persons ostensibly intend to maintain established values. First,
consider the instances of coercion and violence in the Synoptic narratives. In Mark: after his baptism Jesus is *forced* into the wilderness by the
spirit (Mark 1:12//Matt 4:11//Luke 4:1). And soon after, Jesus *drives out*
an unseen, unclean spirit from a possessed man in the synagogue of
Capernaum (Mark 1:25-26//Luke 4:35). The incident implies that
unclean and unseen spirits can do violence to humans, and that some
humans know how to control them. Then, after the healing of the man
with the withered hand, "The Pharisees went out, and immediately held
counsel with the Herodians against him, how *to destroy* him" (Mark

3:6//Matt 9:14//Luke 6:11 RSV). Almost right after that, as crowds gathered so that Jesus and his core group could not even eat, "when his family heard it, they went out *to seize* him, for people were saying, 'He is beside himself'" (Mark 3:21 RSV). Luke, in turn, reports of Jesus' fellow villagers: "When they heard this, all in the synagogue were filled with wrath. And *they rose up and put him out* of the city, and led him to the brow of the hill on which their city was built, that they might *throw him down* headlong" (Luke 4:28-29 RSV). Herod Antipas could on a whim *seize* John the Baptist (Mark 6:17//Matt 14:3//Luke 3:20), and Jesus himself felt free to trespass over presumably well-established social boundaries when "he entered the temple and began *to drive out those* who sold and those who bought in the temple, and he overturned the tables of the money-changers and the seats of those who sold pigeons; and he would not allow any one to carry anything through the temple" (Mark 11:15-16//Matt 21:12//Luke 19:45 RSV). Jesus' close followers would retaliate for shameless inhospitality with fire from heaven (Luke 9:54). Even legitimate authorities (high priests in the Temple area) hold back in the face of the possibility of *violence* against themselves, as Mark notes: "And they tried to arrest him, but feared the multitude, for they perceived that he had told the parable against them; so they left him and went away" (Mark 12:12//Matt 21:46//Luke 20:19 RSV). On the other hand, Mark would have us believe that the authorities continued in their resolve: "And the chief priests and the scribes were seeking *how to arrest* him by stealth, and kill him for they said, 'Not during the feast lest there be a tumult of the people'" (Mark 14:1-2//Matt 26:4//Luke 22:2 RSV). Finally a crowd came and forcibly *seized* Jesus (Mark 14:43-52//Matt 26:47-56//Luke 22:47-53).

John, too, knows of such establishment violence. It is directed toward "public sinners," who are to be *stoned* by command of the law of Moses (John 8:5), hence against Jesus, deemed to fit the divine requirements of such violence (John 10:31-33; 11:8). We are told early on in the narrative that Jesus' opponents sought to *kill* him (John 5:18). Of course Jesus is well aware of their plans (John 7:19-20; 8:37, 40). John's account of Jesus' *arrest, torture,* and *crucifixion* are well known (John 18–19). Similarly, the book of Acts is full of such incidents, beginning with the *arrest* of Peter and John (Acts 4:3), *violence* by unseen agents to Ananias and Sapphira (Acts 5:5-10), the *arrest* of the apostles out of jealousy (Acts 5:18), the council's desire *to kill* them (Acts 6:33), the vigilante treatment of Stephen by a provoked crowd (Acts 7:54-60), and similar instances. For his part, Paul tells us that his fellow Israelites *lashed* him five times, that he was *beaten with rods* three times, and *stoned* once (2 Cor 11:12).

Finally, when we get to the Letter to the Hebrews, we are asked to focus on the blood and gore (Heb 9:7—10:20; 12:4, 24; 13:11–12, 20) so beloved of a society that regales in sacrifice and the endurance of pain that even God is said to use pain as a "fatherly" device for his sons: "do not regard lightly the discipline of the Lord, nor lose courage when you are punished by him. For the Lord disciplines him whom he loves, and chastises every son whom he receives. It is for discipline that you have to endure. God is treating you as sons; for what son is there whom his father does not discipline?" (Heb 12:5-7 RSV; see Pilch 1993a).

By any reading, this was a violent society, with frequent public violence, and unsure and explosive crowd reaction (for the Roman scene, see Brunt 1974). Ordinary persons did not have any rights. There was no universalism in the sense that all human beings were equally human, bearing common human endowments or common human rights independent of individual ethnic origin and social status. Tolerance was an idea whose time would come some seventeen hundred years later! Furthermore, the idea of a plurality of nations endowed with equal rights in the forum of nations was totally absent (perhaps dimly perceived with the Treaty of Westphalia in 1648). International law in the sense of Grotius and his colleagues is rather recent (seventeenth century). Neither ancient Israelites, nor ancient Athenians, nor ancient Romans had any idea of juridical relations among nations. In the first century C.E. Roman statesmen dealt with other ethnic groups in terms of good faith based on patron-client relationships. In Roman perception, Rome was a patron, not a holder of an empire; it wanted persons to behave like clients. To behave otherwise was to be a rebel, an outlaw (see Malina 1992). Neither persons nor nations had rights. What modern readers often interpret as rights is the Mediterranean sense of honor in the political sphere. What I mean is that Roman citizens had preeminence in the *oikoumene*. To dishonor one was to dishonor, to challenge, Rome itself. Consequently, Roman citizens were to be treated honorably by noncitizens: they were not to be flogged publicly, nor were they answerable to any tribunal but that of their own Caesar. Such were the ramifications of the customary values of honor and shame. Persons and nations had no rights, so any modern reader's perception of oppression in the first-century Mediterranean world would be quite anachronistic.

On the other hand, the Mediterranean world was a violent world, and the Israelite tradition hallowed such violence. Philo, the Hellenistic philosopher of Alexandria, clearly explains this tradition (see especially Seland 1995):

> But if any members of the nation betray the honor of the One, they should suffer the utmost penalties . . . all who have zeal for virtue should be permitted to exact the penalties offhand and with no delay, without bringing the offender before jury or council, or any kind of magistrate at all, and give full scope to the feelings which possess them, that hatred of evil and love of God which urges them to inflict punishment without mercy on the impious. They should think that the occasion has made them councilors, jurymen, nome governor, members of assembly, accusers, witnesses, laws, people, everything in fact, so that without fear or hindrance they may champion respect for God in full security. (*Spec. Laws* 1.54; LCL VII:129–30)

Similarly, he notes:

> Further if anyone cloaking himself under the name and guise of a prophet and claiming to be possessed by inspiration lead us on to the worship of the gods recognized in the different cities, we ought not to listen to him and be deceived by the name of prophet. For such a one is no prophet, but an impostor, since his oracles and pronounce-ment are falsehoods invented by himself. And if a brother or son or daughter or wife or a housemate or a friend however true, of anyone else who seems to be kindly disposed, urge us to a like course, bid-ding us fraternize with the multitude, resort to their temples and join in their libations and sacrifices, we must punish him as a public and general enemy, taking little thought for the ties which bind us to him; and we must send round a report of his proposals to all lovers of piety, who will rush with a speed which brooks no delay to take vengeance on the unholy man, and deem it a religious duty to seek his death. For we should have one tie of affinity, one accepted sign of goodwill, namely the willingness to serve God and that our every word and deed promotes the cause of piety. But as for these kinships . . . let them all be cast aside if they do not seek earnestly the same goal, namely the honor of God, which is the indissoluble bond of all the affection which makes us one. (Spec. Laws 1.315–317; LCL; see Räisänen 1986: 287)

Of course he is simply restating the biblical warrant for establishment violence set out in Deuteronomy (Deut 13:5; 13:12–16; 17:2-7, 12; 19:19; 21:21; 22:22, 24; 24:7). When faced with such passages, the problem for the twentieth-century New Testament reader is how to imagine the meanings of the behavior depicted in these writings. What were the explicit and implicit values and meanings presumed by the original author and his audience in the described interaction?

ESTABLISHMENT VIOLENCE: AN OVERVIEW

To talk about the violence depicted in the Synoptic narrative requires at least some set of definitions so that discussion might fruitfully evolve.

> When individuals or groups identifying with the established order defend that order by resorting to means that violate these formal boundaries, they can be usefully classified as vigilantes. . . . [Vigilantism] consists of acts or threats of coercion in violation of the formal boundaries of an established sociopolitical order which, however, are intended by the violators to defend that order from some form of subversion. (Rosenbaum and Sederberg 1976a: 4)

Vigilantism is establishment violence. The foregoing definition would have us adopt the perspective of the hostile crowd and look upon the object of the crowd's hostility as criminal in some way. In the gospel story, Jesus would be the Galilean offender, while in Paul's story, the apostle would be the Judean malefactor.

The violence exerted in establishment violence is socially unendorsed coercion directed by private persons against one another or against the regime. And coercion here is behavior intended to harm a person or a person's values ("The most widely used contemporary definition of politics," says Stettner 1976: 67, is that of David Easton: politics is "the authoritative allocation of values for a society" Easton 1967: 129). Violence transgresses the limits of acceptable coercion; it is aimed at harming another illegitimately. Sederberg notes that considering coercion as "intentional harm" makes sense:

> The degree of harm may vary, and a variety of other purposes may be pursued through the use, or threat, of coercion, just as they may be with other forms of power. The distinguishing characteristic of the use of coercion, though, is intentional harm. . . . Coercion permeates political life, from mild acts of parental discipline to devastating acts

of war. Stable political communities establish and enforce limits on the use of coercion in social relations. Rather than using "coercion," "force," and "violence" interchangeably, we might usefully consider the latter two terms as labels for two types of coercion: Acts of coercion that violate the limits within a particular community may be termed "violence," whereas acceptable coercion may be called "force." The notion of acceptable coercion or force implies a dominant consensus that the benefits of the coercive act outweigh the harm done, as when the police use coercion to apprehend a criminal. (Sederberg 1989: 13)

From the viewpoint of what society considers valuable, violence may be directed to redistributing valuable resources or to maintaining those valuables. When violence is directed to the redistribution of valuables, it is revolutionary or reactionary violence. But when violence is aimed at the maintenance of what society considers valuable, that is, at the maintenance of the status quo, it is vigilantism or establishment violence. From the viewpoint of the object at which the violence is directed, there are three types. First, there is crime-control vigilantism: this is establishment violence that "is directed against people believed to be committing acts proscribed by the formal legal system" (Rosenbaum and Sederberg 1976a: 10). Here the object of crowd hostility is some person or persons who flaunt society's laws by disregarding them, by breaking them. Second, there is social-control vigilantism: this is "establishment violence directed against people believed to be competing for or advocating a redistribution of values within the system" (ibid.: 12). Now the object of the crowd's hostility is a person or group that seeks to alter generally accepted meanings and/or values. This is a form of group social control. Here illegal coercion is a response by those who feel threatened by some mobile segments of society or by those who appear to advocate significant change in the distribution of values. Finally, there is regime-control vigilantism: this is "establishment violence intended to alter the regime in order to make the 'superstructure' into a more effective guardian of the 'base'" (ibid.: 17). Focus here is on controlling the people who are in control. Thus regime-control vigilantism is directed against people in the regime believed to be departing from the established status quo: either forsaking tradition or introducing innovations (see Table 3).

Since vigilante actions are of three types, depending on their purpose (crime-control, group-control, or regime-control), and since participants in such actions may be either private or public individuals, a

TYPE	GOAL	OBJECTS		
Revolutionary or reactionary violence	Alteration of status quo	Propertyholders	Regime	
Establishment violence (vigilantism)	Maintenance of status quo	Deviants (crime control)	Competitors or agents of change (social control)	Innovative rulers (regime control)

TABLE 3
Model of Violence

typology of vigilantism would include six types: public crime-control, group-control and regime-control, and private crime-control, group-control, and regime-control. Questions put to Jesus about his role and purpose might fruitfully be analyzed in terms of the social location of the questioner, public or private, as well as the type of control the questioner might have in mind. Consider the following sampling from Mark in Table 4 (note how priests are public as well as private persons).

All of these types concern the use of violence by established groups to preserve the status quo at times when the formal system of rule enforcement is viewed as ineffective or irrelevant (Bailey 1970 offers a model of political interaction into which vigilantism easily fits; Black-Michaud 1975 brings greater focus to specifically Mediterranean societies; Lewellen 1983 offers a sweeping historical view which locates the previous two works).

PARTICIPANTS	PURPOSES		
	Crime Control	Social Control	Regime Control
Private	Pharisees vs. Jesus (Mark 3:6)	Judeans vs. disciples (Mark 13:9)	Priests vs. Pilate (Mark 15:11-15)
Public	Priests vs. Jesus (Mark 14:1)	Priests vs. Jesus (Mark 12:27-33)	

TABLE 4
Model of Vigilantism

ESTABLISHMENT VIOLENCE
IN THE ROMAN EMPIRE

The foregoing definitions presume that there are indeed formal boundaries of an established social and political order and that there are recognizable procedures and values determining the limits of legitimate coercion. Yet such formal boundaries and procedures were more a set of desiderata than the actual state of affairs in the *oikoumene* of the early Roman imperial period. Any discussion of establishment violence in defense of a social order must, in Mediterranean imperial conditions, distinguish between two value sets—those of the Romans and those of the peoples the Romans sought to assimilate. In Israel, for example, Roman Hellenistic values were fragile, imported values, operating within a situation of relative political imbalance, while Israelite customs formed the indigenous traditional values still exercising profound influence on local ethnic behavior.

Scholars speak generally of the cultural schizophrenia ushered in with Hellenism and its mixture of often conflicting values. On the other hand, the Romans provoked a structural schizophrenia with their Rome-centered, universalistic institutional arrangements imposed upon and/or alongside existing social forms. These cultural and structural imports resulted in a situation of porous and fluctuating social boundaries among many annexed ethnic groups (see Malina 1993: 37)

Thus in the Roman Empire, the universe of values from the viewpoint of local perception was one of cultural dualism: Hellenistic and localite (for example, Israelite). Yet from an empire-wide viewpoint, people saw an *oikoumene* of cultural pluralism (for example, a Roman overlay expressed in Israelite, Athenian, Alexandrian ways). Thus localite cultural dualism involved a juxtaposition of local traditions and a Hellenistic worldview; while cosmopolitan cultural pluralism was implicit in the institutional arrangement of the Roman Empire as Roman officials, temples, and army units appeared alongside local officials, worship forms, and military units. At the local level, the intrusion of Hellenistic values into individual local cultures would be seen as a dualism created and imposed by outsiders (for example, in Sepphoris, Tiberias, and Jerusalem). On the other hand, at the cosmopolite level, the multiplicity of cultures within each Roman province (for example, Hellenistic cities such as Sebaste, Caesarea, and Scythopolis in Palestine replicated in the other *poleis* [cities] of the empire: for example, Alexandria, Damascus,

Antioch) might be seen as the phenomenon of indigenous pluralism. To say that the Roman Empire was a pluralistic *oikoumene* therefore reveals the cosmopolitan perspective. To comment on how Hellenistic values and Roman social structures had permeated towns and villages in Palestine points to a localite perspective. The point is that biblical scholars who comment on the Roman *oikoumene* often adopt the localite perspective for ideological reasons (for example, the uniqueness of Israel, the distinctiveness of Judaism, formation of formative Judaism) while ignoring the other (see Paul 1993: 110-11).

Treatment of vigilantism in the New Testament requires dealing with violence and values. To do so one must thus look at the problems of creating cultural viability in the Roman provinces, specifically in Syria and Judea. For the violence we read about seems directed at deterrence. Individuals and groups decide to deter those who threaten the status quo, be it local, or imperial, or both. And they do so through traditional and acceptable methods of self-help. To whom were such methods of self-help acceptable, and what kind of potential enemies needed deterring?

Significantly, the ancient Mediterranean world surely consisted of people who counted their enemies (Matt 5:43-44; 6:27; Luke 1:71; 19:27, 43). But how much of an enemy to Judeans was a Samaritan in Palestine? an Egyptian in Egypt? a Greek in Asia Minor? How much of an enemy to the Romans was a Judean? Under what conditions would it be acceptable for a Roman to kill a Judean, for a Judean to kill a Galilean, or for an Alexandrian Judean to kill another Alexandrian Judean? How did Mediterranean peoples of the first century distinguish compatriots from hostile aliens, ingroups from outgroups? Much of the violence found in the region was intimately linked to the tensions of cultural pluralism along with the fragile distinction between fellow ethnic, fellow citizen, and alien foe. "Who is my neighbor?" (Luke 10:29, 36 RSV) was hardly a question of religious benevolence and piety! Perhaps the changing contours of ingroup and outgroup boundaries can be glimpsed from the Arabic proverb: "Me against my brother; me and my brother against our cousin; me, my brother and my cousin against our enemies."

The difficulties arising from outwardly imposed dualism and inwardly experienced pluralism are further complicated by different definitions of, hence different perceptions of, the establishment. For example, which establishment and which status quo were focal in the vigilante actions described in the gospels or in Philo? The establishment in the definition of vigilantism refers to "people who prefer things as they are and look with suspicion on any proposal for significant change, whether of a creative or restorative sort" (Rosenbaum and Sederberg 1976b: 266). In first-century Palestine at the local level (and its dualism perceived as outwardly imposed) we find at least a twofold establishment: 1) the native establishment, both visible (local authorities) and invisible (God of Israel, spirits, demons); and 2) the Roman establishment, both visible (prefect, military) and invisible (Roman gods, spirits, and demons, including one named "Legio"). The unseen establishment, for example, included the God of Israel, other gods, as well as the dead ancestors of the tradition, the traditions hallowed by age, the mysterious forces of the night, the commanding power of the elements and the living vitality of the forces of nature: angels, spirits, demons. Gallagher notes "a spectrum of categories ranging from *theos*, the most positive designation, through *anthropos* in the middle, to *magos* and *goēs*, the most negative categories. . . . The space between *theos* and *anthropos*, for example, quickly becomes populated by sons of god, divine teachers, composite beings, demons, famous men of various stripes, wise men, leaders, generals, etc." (1982: 70). The authority of the unseen, of God and a host of nonvisible persons, constitute the Mediterranean's concept of the ultimate. It has a good deal to do with Mediterranean concepts of social causation, of the origins of good and bad fortune, and of the courses of failure and success. (For an excellent description of unseen forces, see Wink 1984.)

Furthermore, in any *polis* of the region, from the Israelite point of view there were invariably two establishments: 1) the Judean ethnic establishment replicated in the Judean quarter of the *polis*; and 2) the prevailing political establishment embracing all the citizens of the city. In these *poleis*, that the offspring of Judean immigrants locally born (the anthropological term is "creoles") both practiced and were the object of establishment violence is quite predictable, for immigrant Judeans (among others) formed pariah communities throughout the region. A pariah community is an ethnic minority that is not indigenous to its host society but has established itself as part of the social system over several generations (von der Mehden 1976: 218). Pariah communities are highly visible minority groups, often with different racial, culinary, religious, and customary features. For various reasons, they tended to include an unusually high proportion of the commercial leadership of the respective host communities. In the contemporary United States, note, for example, the Chinese, Koreans, and Iranians.

Pariah group members are judged stereotypically as rich, avaricious, corrupt, politically opportunistic, subversive at worst and apolitical and antinationalist at best, and, overall, unwilling or disloyal citizens (yet these groups have not been in fact homogeneous and include individuals of different social rank, customs, loyalties, and political opinions). The characteristics of wealth, opportunism, tightly knit kin- (or fictive kin-) based organizations, ambition, opportunism, and cleverness attributed to pariah people have incited jealousy, envy, and fear, resulting in violence not only against those who fit the stereotype, but to the whole community. Judean immigrants entered into commerce in societies where such activities continued to be of low status within the dominant culture. On the other hand, pariah people look on majority culture as composed of people who are lazy, unskilled, and not overly bright (further, see von der Mehden 1976: 229–33). Since pariah groups are readily singled out as not part of the host society and its establishment values, they are often singled out for both scapegoating as well as for vigilantism (hence the noted conflict with Judeans in Alexandria, Rome, and elsewhere).

In practice it might be difficult to distinguish which establishments are involved when people do violence on behalf of the status quo. For example, when the people of the tiny hamlet of Nazareth decide to do away with Jesus (Luke 4:29), who was thought to reach above the level of village equality (see Malina 1993:28–55), or when people came to stone the betrothed suspected of adultery (John 8:1-11), we might say they were enforcing the authority of the visible, local establishment: villagers or Torah groups bent on eliminating potential trouble. Yet when Philo (cited previously) exhorted his co-nationals to vigilante activity should God be dishonored by idolatry, or when Jerusalemites practiced vigilante justice on the Hellenistic Judean Stephen on presumably comparable charges of dishonoring God (Acts 7:58), they sought to deter infraction against the unseen establishment.

The Roman Empire sought to transform the authority of the visible rulers among annexed populations by enforcing local institutions and laws as far as possible. Hellenism, on the other hand, addressed itself to the task of destroying the old traditional invisible authority and replacing it with the alternative authority of a reasonable, invisible Ultimate or with more efficient, helping deities. And yet, on the destructive side, Roman imperialism was more successful than Hellenism. Indigenous institutions of government in the Mediterranean were more or less decisively destroyed, but indigenous belief and value systems were not. Roman architectural structures serve as monuments to the destruction of an old system of social and political control rather than as genuine symbols of a viable new order. Local *decuriones* struggled to find coherence within the institutional void that the Romans produced. To underscore the positive, it was as bringers of Hellenism that Romans were praised, not as broadcasters of Roman institutions. And so, for example, Philo of Alexandria, when writing of Caesar Augustus's conquests in the Alps and in Illyria, stated how the princeps: "had healed the disease common to Greeks and barbarians . . ." (*Embassy to Gaius* 145; LCL). What in fact had Augustus done? "This is he who reclaimed every state (*polis*) to liberty, who led disorder into order, and brought gentle manners and harmony to all unsociable and brutish nations, who enlarges Greece (*Hellas*) with numerous new Greeces and hellenizes (*aphellenisas*) the outside world (*barbaroi*) in its important regions . . ." (147; LCL). So it is not surprising that Paul of Tarsus could write "to the Romans" yet speak only of "Judeans and Greeks" with a passing nod to "Greeks and barbarians" (Rom 1:14). For "Judeans and Greeks," see Rom 1:16; 2:9, 10; 3:9; 10:12; see also 1 Cor 1:24 and passim; Gal 3:28; Col 3:11. This perspective is likewise evidenced in the narrative of Acts (Acts 14:1; 18:4; 19:10-17; 20:21). The social import of "Judeans and Greeks" for Paul and Luke would be "the set apart and the civilized," while Greeks and barbarians meant "the civilized and the uncivilized." Greek writers in general spoke similarly of "Greek and barbarian" (for example, Strabo, *Geography* 1.4.9; LCL).

Hellenism and Roman philosophical systems, on the other hand, did not at all destroy older perspectives. The invocation of God and spirits, special rites for the dead, special bonds of kinship (and the fear of violating those bonds), theories of causation based on unseen factors, and systems of punishment and reward (partly based on invisible convictions) have all survived the massive, normative challenges posed by conquering nations: Persian, Greek, Parthian, and Roman.

Consequently, while Roman institutions of government were basically a facade to disguise what was fundamentally a political grab bag, Hellenism and its belief systems disguised some resilient Mediterranean cultural continuities. Old institutional structures had been destroyed in much of the Roman Empire, but old normative patterns managed to change without dying. And establishment violence was one of these old normative patterns.

Understanding Establishment Violence: A Social Science Approach

In Israel's scriptures, God himself commands the ready use of violence to maintain, defend, or restore the status quo—vigilantism or establishment violence was a cultural given. Among Judean ethnics of the first century, the status quo might be identified with God's honor as in Philo, and the infraction of this honor might provoke "the wrath of God" as in Paul. But most often the status quo is identified with the social position of the agents of vigilantism.

Now there are at least three ways to consider establishment violence. First, it may be considered a procedure for maintaining societal equilibrium. This is the "law and order" view. Establishment violence emerges to maintain the status quo against criminals and sinners. Here laws (including God's revealed laws) are made by those who benefit from the social order in order to maintain their privilege. From this perspective, Jerusalemites would have the criminal Jesus crucified, for example, in order to maintain order in their city and region, for their own benefit. This is the Roman perspective set forth in Luke and John. Thus, Pilate "finds no crime in this man" (Luke 23:4, 22; see John 18:38; 19:4, 6 RSV). The Roman official Gallio is equally concerned with crime in Acts (18:14).

Second, establishment violence may be considered a process whereby moral entrepreneurs seek to defend their interests by exerting control over those who threaten those interests (= benefit maintenance). In this perspective, establishment violence defends the status quo against deviants and subversives. Thus Jerusalem authorities would have found the deviant Jesus advocating a subversive program that would unsettle their interests: political, kin-group, political religious, and political economic. Of course, they believed their interests were those of the whole nation. In the name of those interests, they had Jesus removed. This position is voiced in the well-known statement of Caiaphas in John: "You do not understand that it is expedient for you that one man should die for the people, and that the whole nation should not perish"

(11:50 RSV). We are later told: "It was Caiaphas who had given counsel to the Judeans that it was expedient that one man should die for the people" (John 18:14 RSV).

Finally, establishment violence may be considered a form of communication by which people express outrage at what others say in word and deed. This outrage motivates them to try to restore and reaffirm their meaning of life (= proclaiming cultural meanings). Establishment violence is aimed at restoring the status quo against dissidents and heretics. In this view, Jesus would have been perceived as tampering with Israel's normative discourse and with the purity lines that discourse requires. As heretic, Jesus denied the system that provided meaning for most Judeans and Jerusalemites. They were outraged by what he said and did and therefore, in order to reaffirm the vital meanings Jesus toyed with, they successfully called for his death. Luke expresses this perspective well when he notes: "So they watched him, and sent spies, who pretended to be sincere, that they might take hold of what he said, so as to deliver him up to the authority and jurisdiction of the governor" (20:20 RSV). The various accusations of blasphemy, of injuring God by speech, point to this perspective (see Mark 2:7//Matt 9:3//Luke 5:21; Mark 14:64//Matt 26:25).

Depending on one's theoretical perspective, one may view establishment violence as directed against: 1) criminals and sinners; or 2) deviants and subversives; or 3) dissidents and heretics. In this chapter, I will develop establishment violence scenarios in terms of the three general approaches that define the objects of establishment violence as criminals, deviants, and/or heretics. These are the social-scientific approaches called the structural functionalist approach (producing criminals), the conflictual approach (labeling deviants), and the interpretative approach (declaring heretics).

THE MAINTENANCE OF ORDER:
THE STRUCTURAL-FUNCTIONALIST EXPLANATION

Violent behavior meted out by family to family members, by crowds to fellow citizens or aliens, by unendorsed authorities to opponents, by legitimate authorities illegally, or by unseen persons to unfortunate visible persons, may all be considered procedures for maintaining societal equilibrium. Societal equilibrium is commonly termed "law and order."

To interpret such behavior requires at least two focused looks into the social system in which such behavior makes sense. First, a general perspective on establishment violence will serve to situate that behavior within some comparative framework. Then a more specific perspective outfitted with Mediterranean values will allow for a fuller depiction of the scenario in question.

The fundamental question, though, is: Why vigilante behavior at all? Why do unauthorized people feel constrained to come forward on behalf of the status quo? A structural functionalist approach cannot really explain this feature so readily because structural functionalism presumes societies develop authorized structures to maintain their equilibrium (the status quo). Any intrusion on the part of unauthorized persons would be wanton, vicious, and perverse, hence illegitimate. Further confirmation of this assessment comes from the survey of Stettner (1976: 64–75). Stettner considers the prevailing range of political theories (from naturism to Marxism) and finds that no extant political theory has explanatory room for vigilante behavior. He explains this point largely by arguing that political theory is ethically inspired (ibid.:74) and vigilantism is a political sickness (ibid.: 75). While this may be true, I would say that the reason for this is that political theory building is largely a structural-functional enterprise. Stettner concludes:

> Crime-control vigilantism has been shown to differ quite significantly from social-group control vigilantism and regime control vigilantism in that it does not seem limited to arguing for order and the perpetuation of a favorable status quo. Crime-control vigilantism is a practical response to a short run failure of the legal system to operate "properly." The other types of vigilantism are broader responses meant to supplement or even supplant normal political operations, which may be working too effectively for the tastes of the vigilante group. This is particularly so of social-group control vigilantism. It may be that these phenomena are too diverse to be studied as simply different types of a single kind of political activity. That, at least, would be a possible conclusion to be drawn from looking at vigilantism from the perspectives of political theory. (1976: 75)

The political theory is derived from societies where values and experience match; the behavior of those who live in a society where values and experience do not match is deviance. However, the behavior typical of societies where values and experience mismatch is fully at home in conflict theory.

Furthermore such grand, organic theory derives from hierarchical societies where values and experience usually match (Malina 1986a: 14). They envision systems in which societal values and social experiences in general positively support the expectations of a populace that itself is homogeneous. Such systems were not (and are not) characteristic of the circum-Mediterranean culture area. Furthermore, such systems have little if any room for anomalies. Conflict models and interpretative models are most concerned with such anomalies and best shed light on life in uncertain social environments.

MAINTAINING ONE'S INTERESTS: THE CONFLICT APPROACH

Despite their distinctiveness, the controversies in New Testament narratives have many parallels in general, small-group conflicts. The crucial question to be asked in evaluating such controversies is not how the conflict between the demands of the theocracy envisioned by Jesus and the Torah observance espoused by Pharisees—or between Paul's being in Christ and Judaism's being in Israel—have been resolved. It is rather whether the existing group leadership identified its interests with opposition to particular types of values and value-clusters, especially favoring the imprecise demands of the kingdom of God over precise Torah observance, of the vague being "in Christ" over the precise behaviors required of being "in Israel." How much criticism of traditional values did existing leadership believe could be tolerated at the expense of what was defined as traditional orthopraxy?

From the viewpoint of defending group and personal interests, "vigilantes provided a medium to convey symbolically whose values (those of the propertied) were to prevail in an uncertain social environment" (Little and Sheffield 1983: 806). Thus every act of violence in the gospel story is about whose values are to prevail in a clash of values. It was quite understandable that major value clashes should happen in Jerusalem, especially during festivals that were coupled with pilgrimage. This feature seems to be a Johannine theme (John 2:23; 4:45; 5:1; 6:4; 7:2-14, 37; 10:22; 11:56; 12:12; 13:1; see Malina and Rohrbaugh 1998), although the obviousness of the situation is reported in

Matthew: "Then the chief priests and the elders of the people gathered in the palace of the high priest, who was called Caiaphas, and took counsel together in order to arrest Jesus by stealth and kill him. But they said, 'Not during the feast, lest there be a tumult among the people'" (Matt 26:3-5 RSV). Value clashes were equally common between quarters of ancient cities, whose boundaries were always like frontiers marking off conflicting groups (cf. Philo's *Embassy to Gaius*).

Pilgrimage time is ideal value-conflict time because pilgrims from all parts of the world arrive as relative strangers to each other. The varied local population of the capital city, the increasing heterogeneity of the expanded population, and the resulting differentiation of the people "Israel" in the city—for a time all combined to engender uncertainty about community structure and values and about how choices were to be made among opposed normative systems that were recognized as challenging one another for acceptance and/or dominance. Under these circumstances, crowds turned into violent mobs. Further, vigilante groups emerged to serve the function of dramatizing and affirming the behavioral boundaries of the normative city community, defining and clarifying its structure and supporting establishment values. Vigilantism nearly always has the backing of elite claimants to the status quo, if only because elites alone could readily prosecute deviants, and this well into the nineteenth century. It is important to note with Little and Sheffield that: "Until well into the nineteenth century, criminal prosecution was, practically speaking, readily available only to the wealthy" (1983: 797). In first-century Mediterranean terms, "wealthy" would be high-status persons or the elite; therefore, vigilantism will always reveal a conservative orientation. It picks on the weak, the lowly, the unpopular, people least able to resist or retaliate (Little and Sheffield 1983: 807).

Establishment violence, coalition building, and faction formation are generally found in societies whose governments are rather ineffective in realizing collective goals. Those with a vested interest in the status quo of such societies feel to a greater or lesser extent that the formal institutions of boundary maintenance are ineffective in protecting their interests. The potential for establishment violence on the part of these vested interests is never far below the surface of human interaction: for example, guerrilla bands and warlordism in first-century Palestine (Horsley and Hanson 1985) or twentieth-century Beirut. In this perspective, establishment violence may be considered a process whereby moral entrepreneurs seek to defend boundaries by exerting control over those who threaten those boundaries (= self-help justice and peace maintenance).

Labeling Dissidents

Social systems cannot be fully understood without some attention to the critics who emerge from within them. Similarly, systems based on orthopraxy (as the Judean was or as the Islamic is) cannot be fully understood without some attention to the behaviors that are labeled "deviant" as they emerge in those systems. For example,

> In the abstract, all human societies put some limitations on the exercise of violence. It could even be argued that all human societies regard the act of killing without good cause as immoral. However the definition of what constitutes "good cause" contains an enormous range of variation. Groups that seek to become one political community should learn to narrow that range and incidence of legitimate homicide, if they are to avoid the constant dangers of communal rioting or at least communal tensions. Most countries and societies permit the killing of an "enemy" under certain circumstances. (Mazrui 1976: 195)

In conflict theory, these circumstances are the areas delineated by the respective interests of various groups. "Interest" here means the shared desire of any group of political actors that motivates their political activity. Violence within the bosom of one's group is a heinous crime, while the same behavior at the periphery merits congratulations and reward. And group members perceived to have moved to the periphery are the deviants worthy of vigilante activity.

The role of deviance in the development and perception of correct behavior is central. Social systems are most clearly and systematically articulated when they are formed by negation. The boundaries of what (and who) is right, acceptable, and correct are marked out through a systematic identification of what (and who) is wrong, unacceptable, and incorrect. What people are not to do is often more clearly defined than what they are to do, and it is through battles with deviants that correct behavior is most sharply delineated. Obviously for his opponents, Jesus and his group served as the deviant foil underscoring how not to behave, what not to say, who not to be.

In societies such as those of the first-century Mediterranean, sacred values and behaviors required perpetual defense from destructive forces. Institutional authorities were charged with carrying out the defense, whatever the cost, but in faction-ridden situations, authorities were often remiss. They were more concerned about their own interests than those of the society at large, causing private individuals to see to the maintenance of justice. Since situations in which vigilantism arose were situations of anomaly, often those private individuals looking for "justice for all" were branded as subversive by others (and vice versa). Since such subversives usually believed themselves to have the interests of the sacred institution and tradition at heart, they played an important role in the formation of orthopraxy. Thus one generation's subversive behavior was frequently the next generation's orthopraxy.

The behavior defined as subversive is crucial in the maintenance and transformation of social institutions. Group solidarity is seldom strengthened by anything as much as the existence of a common enemy; note how Herod and Pilate become "friends" over Jesus in Luke 23:12. The subversive is the wayward insider. The identification of subversives shores up the ranks, enables institutional elites to make demands on their subordinates, and reinforces systems of dominance.

In the language register of ideology, such subversives are called heretics. However, it is important to realize that subversion may be part of every social institution, requiring appropriate conflict for its elimination (for example, in politics there are manhunts, in religion there are heresy hunts, in economics there are unfair trader hunts, and in kinship there are feuds and their headhunts). As a form of ideological subversion, the deviance of heretics may be a wrong idea, wrong behavior, or wrong speech (for wrong speech, see below).

It is important to note that the deviance called "heresy" is rarely, if ever, created by "heretics." Rather heresy is nearly always created by the establishment. Specifically, the heresy creator is a representative of the establishment who plays the role of "moral entrepreneur."

> The moral entrepreneur is a person privy to the making and enforcing of societal rules. Rule making is a moral enterprise—a process of constructing and applying meanings that define persons and their behaviors as morally adequate or not. The moral enterprise is an interpretation of a person, requiring both the making of rules (rule creator) as well as the application of rules to specific persons (rule enforcer). The moral entrepreneur is the person likely to initi-

ate a deviance process and to mobilize the forces necessary to make it successful. All right minded people will be expected to subscribe to the culturally specific and highly emotionally charged goals selected by the entrepreneur. And it is specifically these sorts of goals that the moral entrepreneur espouses. The moral entrepreneur becomes socially unassailable, unless opponents can redefine the situation by neutralizing the constraint unassailability produces. As rule creators moral entrepreneurs and their followers wish to interpret some behavior as deviant for the purpose of obviating, preventing or correcting interferences in their interests. They wish to change, enforce or establish rules to these ends. They do so by defining both certain conditions and those who engage in those conditions as inimical to their values and interests—personal, group and societal. (Malina and Neyrey 1988:43–44)

Thus the deviance called heresy results from the work of moral entrepreneurs, their following, and their organization by means of a process of: 1) diagnosing opposition values as all pervasive; then 2) labeling those who espouse those values as subversive deviants; and eventually 3) articulating a counter position (= orthodoxy) requiring counter behavior (orthopraxy) or insisting on counter speech forms (ortholoquy).

Vigilantism is establishment violence against a person or persons successfully labeled as deviant by some moral entrepreneur in the community for the purpose of maintaining prevailing values. The moral entrepreneur perceives common values as being impugned (criminal-control vigilantism), rearranged (group-control vigilantism), or ignored by those whose task is to see to their enforcement (regime-control vigilantism). The object of vigilantism is to eliminate deviant behavior. Deviance theory focuses upon the process by which a normal person becomes a deviant—the labeling process. There are, of course, a number of ways of dealing with deviant persons: ignoring them, tolerating them, applying legitimate coercion, and applying illegitimate coercion.

Hierarchically structured societies—societies in which value expectations and value capabilities match—normally feature legitimate coercion in face of subversion; all opposition is deviant. But uncertain social environments typical of societies in which value expectations and value capabilities do not match usually feature some form of vigilantism; here opposition activity is viewed as depravity, hence as deviance (see Malina 1986b). Gurr makes the same point: "The value expectations of a collectivity are the average value positions to which its members believe they are justifiably entitled ... The value capabilities of a collectivity are the average value positions its members perceive themselves capable of attaining or maintaining" (1970: 27). Further, "in the special case of vigilante violence, a singular type of deprivation appears to be operative: 'decremental deprivation.' This occurs when value expectations of groups remain fairly constant, but perceived value capabilities decline. The more precipitous this decline, the greater potential for violence by the 'deprived' group" (Rosenbaum and Sederberg 1976a: 5–6, citing Gurr 1970: 46–50).

Vigilante theory focuses upon the one type of coercion applied to dealing with the phenomenon of subversion and/or deviance: violence ("illegitimate coercion directed by private persons against one another or against the regime may be defined as violence" Rosenbaum and Sederberg 1976a: 3–4). Legitimate coercion directed by a private person (for example, the difference between disciplining a child and child abuse) or legitimate coercion by a public person (for example, the difference between police coercion and police brutality) are not violence, but simply coercion.

Vigilantism looks to the suppression of subversion by eliminating subversives. Subversion has both an intellectual content, the point at issue, as well as a social dimension, the critic and the criticized (the orthopractical and the deviant). People commit themselves to particular definitions of worldviews and symbol systems not only because they make sense intellectually but also because those definitions of reality resonate with, or have an affinity with, the interests and lifestyles of those choosing them. Both Jesus and his opponents, for example, defined Torah obedience in ways that served their respective interests and then gave to their definitions the aura of objective truth and universality, whether localite or cosmopolitan.

LABELING THRESHOLD

Institutional responses to subversion derive from the interplay of the social distance between the statuses of subversives and institutional authorities on the one hand and the ideational distance between the beliefs of subversives and those of elites on the other.

First consider social distance. Criticism from within a social organization is more intellectually offensive than external criticism. Deviant insiders are more of a direct threat than external critics who are outside agitators and can be defined off the scale of relevant persons and easily dismissed as "not one of us." As for ideational distance, the criticisms of internal opponents (subversives) operating on identical internal assumptions are more dangerous to those in power than critiques that operate from extrinsic assumptions.

If these perspectives are on target, then mechanisms of control will be activated by elites only when social distance and ideational distance reach, but do not exceed, a critical level. If either is too high or too low, they may be ignored. In the case of Torah observers, the question is when to activate the Torah rule: to kill the idolater, stone the adulteress, eliminate the recalcitrant child, do away with the false prophet.

In institutionalized belief systems, those in charge come to define and articulate the values of the system, thereby attaching their interests to those definitions and articulations. Social conflict concerning those values leads to redefinitions and new articulations—thus the parties to the conflict define their interests in terms of the system. For example, the political religion of Judea became the preserve of the high priesthood and the Sanhedrin: the high priesthood and Sanhedrin defined and articulated the values of the system and attached their interests to those definitions and articulations. Eventually the interests and status of Pharisee council members and of the burgeoning scribal bureaucracy of Jerusalem became attached to and associated with the prestige of the high priesthood and the doctrine on which it was based. It was when opposing ideas threatened those interests that the instinct of self-preservation in the ruling stratum reacted by attaching the stigma of deviance or subversion. Then the high priesthood and Sanhedrin members, either scribal bureaucrats or Pharisees, would be quick to affix the stigma of deviance on opponents.

In this context, deviance is the subversion of one who, having been born and claiming membership in a given community or society, continues to behave in a way contrary to the values that one is under obligation of local ethical affiliation to follow in practice. At times this local ethical affiliation is ethnic (all members by birth are expected to follow it; for example, Judeans, Romans, Cretans), fictive ethnic (all members by fictive or ritual birth are expected to follow it; for example, Christians, Stoics, Isis cultists), or political (all members are expected to follow it by law or custom; for example, Corinthians, Romans, Judeans).

PROCLAIMING THE MEANING OF LIFE:
THE INTERPRETIVE APPROACH

Finally, establishment violence may be considered a form of communication whereby people say things about themselves and others, thus expressing the meaning of some significant aspect of life in face of the denial or alteration of that meaning. In the interpretive approach, people do things to "mean" to others. In the case of violence done to another, such violence requires that the other be redefined as inhuman so that he or she might be treated as such. For example, dissidence has to be viewed as essentially having dehumanized the dissident, who may henceforth be dealt with as nonhuman. Such redefinition has to do with the lines that constitute the purity system, as well as the exclusive dimensions of those lines that constitute the sacred. When viewed through the prism of the prevailing purity system, the dissident is seen clearly as outside the realm of what is holy and exclusive to the group. The dissident stands in the area of the hostile. In the area of the hostile, wrong (that is, dissident) ideas, speech, and behavior abound; it is the realm of heterodoxy, heteroloquy, and heteropraxy, and thus of the choices (*haireseis*) that mark dissidence. Dissidents thus come to serve as a symbolic focus for moral entrepreneurial attack on the subversive forces responsible for the many problems of the group or society to which the moral entrepreneur belongs.

DISSIDENCE AND SPEECH

From a symbolic viewpoint, what constitutes a dissident? Dissidence can be considered as essentially a semiotic phenomenon, employing either speech or behavior or both, which communicates to and results in cognitive disorientation for "true" believers. The conflict among Judean groups carried on in the first-century Mediterranean was essentially about divine power revealed in political power. This is what political religion— religion embedded in the political institution—is about. In Palestine, embedded political religion was the means used by competing factions "in Israel" to appropriate the world for their own purposes and gratification, for their own interests. Outside of the Israelite homeland, embedded kinship religion (see Malina 1986b) was the means by which first-century immigrant and creole Judean groups sought to appropriate the world into which they and their forebears migrated. A dissident attempted similar use of available means, but for his own interests. And the chief tool used by such dissidents was speech, communicative acts in a broad sense. They sought to control the discourse (see Zito 1983, on whom this discussion is based).

A dissident is perceived by the establishment to challenge the prevailing monopoly of his group's interpretation of reality. His challenge consists of articulating another interpretation of reality in terms of the same premises shared by the group. Such articulation might be called "heteroloquy" (after the pattern of heterodoxy and heteropraxy). Heteroloquy is a dissident way of talking about events and processes (after Zito 1983: 123, who calls this heresy). Every social institution as well as each society as a whole may be characterized by or as a specific discourse.

"Discourse" here means any collective activity that orders its concerns through language. Examples of discourse include academic disciplines, national political systems, denominational belief systems. As a rule, prevailing discourse tends to be an ideology, a discourse seeking to monopolize ways of speaking about the world. The usual course of social interaction, then, is "ortholoquy." Ortholoquy refers to expressing oneself in language (spoken and written) in terms of the institutionalized ideology. It is the received way of speaking and writing about, hence of expressing, received views. The set of received views would constitute the prevailing orthodoxy, and behavior based on these views would be the prevailing orthopraxy.

In this perspective, "heteroloquy" is any way of speaking that upsets, or at least threatens to upset, an institutionalized way of speaking. And since people speak with goods as well as with other nonverbal behavior, communications through these means that upset or at least threaten the institutionalized way of speaking is equally heteroloquy; for example, giving all one's goods to the poor. Heteroloquy is dissidence; heteroloquy is subversiveness.

Consider the language used in the United States relative to contemporary Israel. Israeli squatters are called "settlers"; Israel's army of occupation is called a "defense force"; Israel's theft of Palestinian property is called a "return"; Israel's racist anti-Gentilism is called "Zionism"; and any and all criticism of Israel's chosen people behavior is labeled "anti-Semitism"!

The dissident status of my language in the previous paragraph is determined by the institutionalized legitimization of the discourse within which the dissidence is voiced. In this case the legitimate discourse institutionalized in the United States is the very discourse of

Israel itself, as unbelievable as that might be! Dissidence threatens established power relations. Should my discourse prevail, the United States would have to cut funding to Israel on moral grounds, thus appreciably weakening the occupiers of Palestine.

Dissidence, as my statements indicate, is in essence a semiotic phenomenon employing meaningful signs that result in cognitive disorientation of true believers (Zito 1983: 125). Israelis and Christian fundamentalists in the United States find my statements quite disorienting; as a matter of fact, they are sufficient to label me "an enemy of Israel," or, more derogatorily, "an anti-Semite."

Now what is essential to heteroloquy is the cognitive disorientation of true believers. Such cognitive disorientation produces in the faithful a cry of outraged hostility (note the endless letters to the editor in countless newspapers and journals upon any hint or illusion of tampering with Israel's control of the discourse, such as calling Hizbollah "freedom fighters"!). It is the outrage provoked by communicative behavior—words and actions—that ultimately counts. In this perspective, what is worth analyzing in establishment violence is what did the dissident communicate in word and/or deed to provoke the outrage.

> What we recognize in a statement as heretical is its ability to produce in the faithful a cry of outraged hostility. This had led in the past to vindictive persecution of the heretic, who is then literally or figuratively burned at the stake. A collective response is invoked that sometimes leads the community to betray, although always in the name of collective unity, the very principle that is at stake in the first place. The true believers sense that in some way their innermost selves have been violated, their moral values usurped, their very existence as a moral community placed in jeopardy. (Zito 1983: 126)

In this regard, if Jesus is accused of dissidence, of heteroloquy, then he must have violated the innermost selves of his opponents as well as those of the Jerusalem crowd. Their reaction indicates that he usurped their moral values and placed their existence as a moral community in jeopardy. Zito further notes:

> It may be, of course, that it is the likelihood of some deviant, nonnormative activity implied but unstated by the heretic which constitutes the greatest threat: the true believer may be able to project the possible consequences of the heretical statement and be appalled at

what he finds. An imaginary deviance may appear more gross and blasphemous than an actual deviance, particularly if the latter is "only words." Historically this seems to have been the case, as an examination of religious heresies clearly indicates. (Zito 1983: 126)

Thus heteroloquy that provokes establishment violence is a dissident way of speaking about the world and its value objects that causes outrage in some hearer(s). Some authoritative moral entrepreneurs enjoying prominence in a community have to label such statements as discordant discourse, as deviant (in my example: as "anti-Semitic," the pan-Israeli putdown). In this way the labeled heteroloquy becomes an attack—once veiled but now quite open—upon an institutionalized way of speaking about the world. Further, the outrage may be caused by what is actually said and done as well as by what is actually not said and not done and by implications perceived as unwholesome consequences. If we admit x, then y and z are sure to follow. If Israel is a racist state, then cuts in funding and rejection by democratic states are sure to follow.

In any case, heteroloquy (heterodoxy, heteropraxy, heresy) are always rooted in and derive from the ideology of the group. Heteroloquy brings out the possible implication for deviance in the shared ideology. Dissident statements are always based upon prevailing discourse, yet they lead to quite different consequences than one's faith has led one to expect. Zito offers the following examples:

Zionism is racism. Feminism is sexism. Equal opportunity is anti-egalitarian. University graduates are not educable. The first mistake of U.S. foreign policy was the American revolution. Marx suffered from false consciousness. Freud had sex problems. (Zito 1983:126)

Of course the list may be expanded to include: The sincere reading of the Bible is the root of fundamentalistic intolerance. Private property causes socialism. Respect for superiors develops authoritarian personalities. Delaying marriage to adulthood causes sexual profligacy. *Das Kapital* is a Marxist-Leninist fetish, and so on.

Each of these statements is, or can be, heteroloquy, and for the following reasons: First, each can be rationally defended in terms of the same ideology that produced its opposite. Second, each threatens to disrupt some ideologically vested power position and has possible consequences in terms of action. Third, each is framed for some institutional context. Fourth, each provokes surprise or outrage among true believers but laughter or indifference among outsiders. In this, heteroloquy statements are like ethnic jokes, only like ethnic jokes told by outsiders and heard by an ethnic because, among themselves, insiders laugh at ethnic jokes or are indifferent to them.

Among the statements of Jesus in the gospel story, some are direct challenges: He tells some Pharisees and their scribes: "You brood of vipers! How can you speak good, when you are evil? For out of the abundance of the heart the mouth speaks" (Matt 12:34 RSV). And again he labels them "an evil and adulterous generation" (Matt 12:39; 16:4; Mark 8:38 RSV). For persons who traced their honor to Abraham by pure genealogy, to be called "snake bastards" and "wicked bastards" should provoke irrevocable enmity. The same two categories are the objects of the series in Matt 23:13-29 with the refrain: "How shameless you are, scribes and Pharisees, hypocrites!" Then consider the "woes" leveled at various elites in the population: "But how shameless you are, you that are rich . . . How shameless are you, you that are full now . . . How shameless are you, you that laugh now . . . How shameless you are, that all men speak well of you" (Luke 6:24-26; translation after Hanson 1996).

Such challenges to honor are not heteroloquy. They really do not disturb the prevailing ideology. Such is not the case with a statement such as "Your sins are forgiven," with its intimation of knowledge of God's activity (Mark 2:9//Matt 9:2//Luke 5:20; 7:48). Similarly, statements such as "how honorable are the [you] poor" (Matt 5:3; Luke 6:20) would displace divine approval from the elites to the socially dishonored, resulting in quite a tear in the prevailing discourse. And a statement such as "But many that are first will be last, and the last first" (Mark 10:31; Matt 19:30 RSV) would overturn the social fabric, if taken seriously. Likewise to advise that social reconciliation has primacy over temple sacrifice as in: "Leave your gift there before the altar and go; first be reconciled to your brother, and then come and offer your gift" (Matt 5:24 RSV) is to tamper with prevailing ideology. And the same holds for the statement: "What comes out of a man is what defiles a man" (Mark 7:20; Matt 15:18 RSV).

A final point to observe concerns the difference between heretics and apostates. Heretical dissidents speak the same language used in prevailing discourse. They can be and are understood. Jesus could be and was understood by his contemporaries, but hardly by ours. For this reason heresy is a type of heteroloquy. On the other hand, apostate dissidents speak a language different from prevailing discourse; they simply cannot be understood, hence are best ignored (perhaps those speaking the language of John's gospel belong here). To be creditable, a dissident must always appeal to those same values that enable the prevailing ortholoquy to maintain its monopoly on the values. When the guardians of ortholoquy are remiss in their duty, establishment violence will emerge to restore cognitive certitude and to assuage outrage.

CHARACTERISTICS OF DEVIANT DISSIDENTS

People in a given society view subversives and dissidents as standing for the intimate union of inside and outside, of within and without, of nearness and remoteness (see Kurtz 1983 on these characteristics). Jesus and his disciples, for example, were open to sinners and nonsinners alike. Similarly, Paul and his "in Christ" group members welcomed Israelite and foreigner alike. Such openness utterly confuses commitment or loyalty or solidarity boundaries. If only for this reason, subversives must be obliterated and eliminated. They are within the group, circle, or institution, therefore close enough to be threatening, but distant enough to be considered wrong, unacceptable, incorrect, evil. The heretic, then, is always a wayward insider (only insiders or those in covenant or kin relations can be tempted or tested). Subversives are traitors in the camp, people without commitment to those other fellow humans who form the society of the subversive's natural birth or legal birth. Subversive behavior always bears a close resemblance to orthopraxy: Jesus could pass for John the Baptist, Elijah, or one of the prophets (see Mark 8:28), even though in the end he was judged to be subversive. It is developed within the framework of orthopraxy and is claimed by its proponents to be truly correct, acceptable, and proper. Like the subversive, subversion itself is both near and remote at the same time.

A second characteristic of subversive behavior is that its meaning derives from interpretations developed in the course of conflict. The interests or duties (they are identical) of conflicting parties become attached either to a defense of alleged subversion or to the condemnation of it. These interests or duties encode the values of the moral entrepreneurs who come forth against the subversion and the values of those accused of subversion—themselves moral entrepreneurs in favor of questioning the boundaries marked off by the existing value set. The problem of subversion, therefore, is essentially a problem of legitimating peripheral or supporting values in terms of a commonly shared set of core values.

Subversion has social consequences, often of a positive sort. It is not only disruptive, but can be used for the creation of intragroup solidarity and for social control. Through the dissidence process, moral entrepreneurs—as public professors of institutional values—can rally support for their positions through battle with a common enemy. Note how Barabbas and his cause get accepted by the chief priests and the Jerusalemite crowd thanks to the envy of the elites in their opposition to Jesus (Mark 15:6-14).

Often, then, institutional elites, as moral entrepreneurs, are actually involved in the formation of subversive movement groups. They do so first by beginning to portray a trend of behavior in a particular way, defining it as having a form, substance, and consistency that it might not have had until suggested by the elites. For example, in the Markan story line, Jesus heals: he exorcises, restores health, and assures people that God forgives them; the fact that Pharisees and monarchist Herodians decide Jesus has to be killed (Mark 3:6) indicates that his behavior was interpreted as an assertion of power over the polity, a Messianic ploy. Then, adherents of questionable views may be driven together to form a movement for their common defense against an attack on their views by institutional elites. For example, again in Mark, the Pharisees and Herodians, often at odds, joined forces to kill Jesus in Mark 3:6, only to be egged on and, of course, coopted by the Temple authorities in Mark 12:12-13.

The process of labeling subversion has both ideological as well as behavioral consequences. The articulation of orthopraxy is formulated in the heat of conflict, often through explicit disagreement with a position held by subversives, at times at the expense and at times for the benefit of the social system in question. In the Synoptic storyline, the authors underscore increasing disagreement between Jesus and the defenders of orthopraxy from the beginning to the end (Mark 2:16-17 and 11:27-33). As positions polarize and people choose sides, it becomes increasingly difficult to be tolerant and allow choices among positions that have conflicting political implications. So in the end, the Jerusalem authorities "tried to arrest him, but feared the crowd" (Mark 12:12

NRSV), so they awaited a more favorable opportunity. Therefore, to understand and interpret orthopraxy and orthodoxy, the historical contexts in which they were formed and the types of subversives that arose in opposition to them must be understood.

Moreover, the process of defining and denouncing subversion and subversives as deviant is a ritual (Malina and Neyrey 1988). Most rituals serve to relieve anxiety and so does the suppression of subversion.

> Rituals serve to relieve social and psychological tensions and to focus anxiety on that which is controllable. Anxiety over the weather is channeled into anxiety over the proper performance of weather-oriented rituals such as the rain dance. Anxiety over longevity can be translated into concern over keeping certain religious commandments ("That it may go well with thee and that thou mayest prolong thy days upon the earth" [Deut 4:40]). (Kurtz 1983: 1090–91)

As with the rain dance, it is not clear that the denunciation of subversion is effective in fulfilling the explicit purpose of the ritual. Nonetheless, such denunciations provide ritual occasion for authorities to do something about the difficulties the social group is facing. In the Gospels, the ritual of status degradation to which Jesus is subject simply underscores the difficulties faced by elite Judean corporate groups— Sadducees, Pharisees, and Herodians—in the face of Roman institutional dominance.

So vigilantism as ritual points to anxieties and/or difficulties that group members are facing at the boundaries of their ingroup. The ritual rationalizes hate, underscores differences, and celebrates the commitment or loyalty which vigilante group members feel for and owe each other. As for who will be singled out by vigilante moral entrepreneurs for their rituals, we might note with Kurtz (ibid.: 1091) that "there is also a certain negative aspect of affinities between ideas and interests in that certain foes are ideal foes." Thus new prophets and their messages were the ideal subversives for the Judean establishment to attack, and those disobedient to old prophecy were the ideal foes for the opponents. Similarly, Judean particularism, replicated in the henotheism of the *Shema* ("Your God" Deut 6:4), a "Chosen People" ideology, and separationist "kosher" practices, was the ideal deviance for non-Judeans to attack, while idolatry, replicating Hellenistic pluralism and "catholicism," was the ideal foe for Judeans.

Conclusion

Establishment violence is always an expression of concern for maintaining the social situation the way it is. Those who participate in establishment violence are called vigilantes. Vigilantes have a firm commitment to the status quo and wish to keep it untouched and inviolate.

Like patronage, clientelism, coalition building, and faction formation, establishment violence is also generally found in societies with uncertain social environments. Governments are often ineffective in realizing collective goals on behalf of the general populace. Violence by established groups to preserve the status quo emerges at times when the formal system of rule enforcement is viewed as ineffective or irrelevant. Life in such a society is characterized by deception, uncertainty, precariousness. Hence, anything seeming to threaten the status quo of elites will catch the attention of moral entrepreneurs. Persons responsible for the threat will be labeled criminals, subversives, or dissidents, and made the ready target of establishment violence. Such was the world of the New Testament.

So long as Jesus confined his work to Galilee and so long as the Galilean crowds supported him, it seems he had nothing to fear from elites. This is because a low profile, along with admiration by a large-enough outgroup, would prevent a presumably deviant person or group from becoming the target of violence. But should the person's or group's profile become too prominent—or should they lose admiration in the eyes of the broader outgroup—vigilante justice would be only a matter of time and occasion. So once Jesus' Galilean success spilled over into Judea, and once the Jerusalemite crowds withdrew their support, elites could restore the status quo by eliminating Jesus. People divinely put on the prowl for subversives and deviants will cultivate establishment violence. In summary, we can say that sporadic conflict in the ancient Mediterranean (often labeled anti-Judaism or persecution of Christians) was typical. That this conflict emerged as establishment violence was predictable. Only time and occasion were unknown. It seems the fates of Jesus and his followers were not out of the ordinary, given the social context.

Early on in Mark's story of Jesus, we are told that exclusivist Pharisees and monarchist Herodians "held counsel . . . against him, how to destroy him" (Mark 3:6). This, of course, is vigilantism. From what precedes this decision, it is apparent that Pharisee groups reacted with "crime control" vigilantism of a deviant (alleged prophet breaking the Sabbath and eating with tax collectors and sinners), while the Herodians took up "group control" vigilantism of an agent of political change (alleged prophet proclaiming theocracy against monarchy). Both streams flow together as the story of Jesus unfolds. But the undercurrent of vigilantism is always quite near the surface.

Roman funerary relief, Pergamon Museum, Berlin

∾ 3 ∾

HIDDEN SOCIAL
DIMENSIONS
OF THE KINGDOM

The kingdom of God proclaimed by Jesus was a political institution in which religion and economics were embedded. To understand Jesus' proclamation as it was perceived by his audience requires a basic set of scenarios—some sort of explicit consideration of the ways that people understood themselves and their relationships. Living with others inevitably entails a perception of how one's life is controlled by others and how to approach those others who control one's life. This perception of being controlled and the perception of connection to the controllers is fundamental to the social institution of politics as well as to religion. Religion is always rooted in analogies drawn from the social experience of being controlled and of connection to those who control, whether in a kinship or in a political framework.

To obviate anachronistic assessments of political religion in New Testament times, we can situate the institution of religion within the framework provided by the stages of social bonding. The history of religion as institution can be articulated in the following way. Originally, religion was embedded exclusively in kinship. There was only domestic religion because, in a presumed tribal organization, all social institutions were undifferentiated and coterminous, therefore embedded in a kinship matrix that formed the tribe. Subsequently, religion was embedded in both kinship and politics. The rise of central administrative places—preindustrial cities—saw the differentiation of the kinship group from the political institution. Perhaps a specialized kin-group handled collective effective action for the entire population. With this differentiation, religion took two forms: kinship religion and political religion. Finally, with further differentiation resulting in the disembedding of religion to become a freestanding institution, the separation of "church and state" is conceivable. The same stages are true of economics as institution. It too was embedded exclusively in kinship, then in kinship and politics, and then disembedded to become a freestanding institution.

What were the social pathways that allowed people to interact in the political sphere, the sphere of social control? In other words, how were people expected to act toward those who controlled their existence in an empire or a kingdom or a city? What analogies would these experiences produce for understanding how God controlled his people, for how the kingdom of God worked? Recently James (1992) proposed an appropriate model for what he calls "abstract community." His model describes three stages, from tribe to kingdom to nation. Each stage marks a change in the relationship between the controllers and the controlled. James calls the change ontological, a radical step-level change. The purpose of these considerations is to use James's contribution to develop a typology of the main modes of social control in vogue in the New Testament period in order to compare them with the main modes employed in our own day. I focus solely on the New Testament period and today, since my task is to elaborate a comparative social-scientific model for understanding Jesus' proclamation of the kingdom of God. For persons unaccustomed to thinking abstractly, such a typology might seem a bit presumptuous since it will encompass two thousand years and more of quite varied cultural experience. After all, are not human beings infinitely and indefinitely varied and variable? From the viewpoint of idiosyncratic and individualistic psychology, that undoubtedly seems true, at least for people enculturated in individualistic ways (see Triandis 1989). But the typology I wish to present is a social one, and human social forms, like human social institutions, are quite limited in number (see Turner 1991).

The value of such a comparative model is that it renders explicit the often invisible lenses through which we at the start of the twenty-first century consider our world. The model equally allows us to put on another set of lenses with which to view the world of Jesus and our ancestors in Christian faith. With these "control" lenses in place, I will consider religion as it would look in the first century and how it looks today.

MODES OF SOCIAL CONTROL

It is common knowledge that social interaction in the ancient Mediterranean followed the pathways of face-to-face living for the most part,
with the vast majority of the population living in villages. Greene offers
the following assessment:

> An important observation which has emerged from fieldwork stud-
> ies of the Roman countryside in Spain, Gaul, Britain and Syria is the
> peripheral nature of towns, which indicates that a wide range of
> trading transactions must have been conducted in rural markets. Of
> course, ancient historians have stressed for some time that no sharp
> division really existed between urban and rural life, and that their
> separation is an intrusive concept from the medieval period or the
> modern industrialised world. In the Mediterranean area, substantial
> sections of the populations of many towns have farmed the sur-
> rounding areas from their urban base right up to the present day. Lit-
> erary sources make it clear that wealthy Romans owned large town
> houses and also country estates; in the provinces, some administra-
> tive capitals may have held that role not because of any intrinsic
> importance, but because they were located at a convenient meeting-
> place for the wealthy members of the town council, the curia. Recent
> archaeological research in the gardens of Pompeii and the "black
> earth" of London has demonstrated that the division between town
> and country should be blurred even further, both in early Roman
> Italy and late Roman Britain. (Greene 1986: 140)

Peter Brown observes that: "The 'face-to-face' community is the unit
of Late Antique religious history" (Brown 1978: 3), and perhaps even
earlier in Mediterranean history. But what is the meaning of a "face-to-
face community" with its characteristic face-to-face social control?

Perhaps the best way to imagine such a social structuring of relationship and the meaning it generates is to situate face-to-face social interaction within the series of modes of interaction that eventually emerged in
European history. James, in his analysis of the historical modes of political institutionalization, notes three significant and step-level changes. He
labels these sequential changes: face-to-face, agency-extended, and disembodied-extended relations. The question is: How did those controlling
others in the polity affect the persons they controlled? First, in a tribal
setting, face-to-face social relations were quite normative in social

interactions. Then, with the rise of feudal kingdoms in the European Middle Ages, an agency-extended mode emerged typified by the presence of agents or middlemen interacting on behalf of significant persons, from pope and king down. Finally, about 250 years ago, with the emergence of the nation-state, a new mode arose, characterized by James as the disembodied-extended mode. In this last mode individuals interact with no actual person at all, but only with disembodied extensions of significant persons as presented in various media, beginning with print, and followed by radio, film, television, videocassette messages, and so on.

In summary, characteristic forms of ingroup political interaction from tribe to kingdom to nation-state have become increasingly abstract even though, as each form emerges, it seems truly "concrete" to those socialized in the form (James 1992: 335). We, for instance, consider television images to be concrete representations of reality; when we watch and listen to a presidential address, we believe the president is actually, concretely, speaking to us. Of course, we are experiencing electric impulses, not a real person. For mnemonic reasons, I would label the forms of political control set out by James as 1) face-to-face; 2) face-to-mace; and 3) face-to-space. The first describes interaction with someone who personally exerts direct control, whether symbolically (through authority) or physically (through force). This form of control does not disappear in subsequent periods. What does happen, though, is that it ceases to be the prevailing or characteristic mode in the political institution of the society. Eventually, face-to-face interaction gave way to the second mode in which the politically controlled interacted with persons serving as agents for those wielding authority. These agents brandish a "mace"—at times metaphorical, at times not—for those in control. Finally, an interactive mode emerged involving no "body" at all—just squiggles on a printed page, lights on a projection screen, electrons coursing over the face of a television set, or pixels on a computer screen. With this last mode, persons wielding political authority control by making their directives known by means of disembodied media; after all, it is not their personal authority that they wield, but that of "the people."

James explains that agency-extended forms of control and interaction (what I call face-to-mace) actually emerged "in a quasi-regulated way in feudal Europe" (James 1992: 322). For biblical scholars, this poses a problem. How might one characterize the mode of control that we all learn about with the emergence of various imperial systems before the European feudal period (for example: Assyrian, Babylonian, Persian,

Hellenistic, Roman)? Those systems were no longer characterized by the face-to-face forms of tribal groups. And yet, as James indicates, these empire systems did participate in some of the features of feudal agency-extended social formations. However, the key characteristic that he notes for the agency-extended mode is that representatives or agents of central institutions, including clerics and tax collectors, came to administer to geographically separated groups of people who, at the face-to-face level, continued to have few points of connection with other groups. These representatives or agents served the institution, the monarchy, the church.

To serve monarchy or church is to serve a personification, that is, to serve the institution personified. It seems to me that this is the central difference between the feudal agency-extended form and previous forms. For ancient emperors did utilize agency-extended forms of control, only with this difference from the medieval form: In antiquity the agents served emperors not empires; they served a specific monarch, not the monarchy. Thus with a change of kings, former staff and clients "fall from grace" or must establish new relations (see 1 Kgs 2:1-9). In the Roman Empire, the Roman bureaucracy was the *familia Caesaris*, not some enduring "civil service." The emperor's role toward his ingroup was that of patron; what he bestowed was favor and persons who facilitated access to the emperor were brokers or intermediaries (see Millar 1977). Since the modes of political control and access to controllers in vogue during the pre-New Testament period and during the New Testament period were essentially patronage-oriented, and since agents were in fact intermediaries or brokers, I would call this mode broker-extended. Patronage essentially "kin-ifies" relations—simulating kinship or creating fictive kinship—between the controlled and those in control (see Malina 1988). So the institutionalization of patron-client relations would mark a meaningful movement from face-to-face kinship-embedded politics to a new form. This form was politics disembedded from kinship; it was a freestanding patronage politics. What the controlled populace sought was favor (Latin: *gratia;* and Greek: *charis*), never rights, since they had none. In the mnemonic sequence I previously suggested, I would call this second stage (of four, now) "face-to-grace," with "grace" meaning favor or patronage.

Face-to-face interactions presuppose actual or fictive kinship bonds with one's family and village mates. Face-to-grace interactions are based on common clientelistic relations with one's fellow fictive and non-fictive ethnics in an *oikoumene* under the control of a patron, hence with a politically central personage with whom one might have fictive kin ties. Face-to-mace, agency-extended interactions are based on comradeship with fellow subjects of a local king or bishop, with fellow worshippers of a local god, vertically associated in a hierarchy of lesser and higher kings, bishops, and sacred places. Finally, face-to-space, disembodied-extended interactions look to fellow citizenship with a national mass of permanently anonymous strangers. While all four forms of social interaction exist in the contemporary world, such was not the case in Mediterranean antiquity. (For an extensive comparison, see Table 4.)

MODES OF POLITICAL SOCIAL INTERACTION: AN OVERVIEW

The contemporary nation-state is actually less than 250 years old. Yet that form of polity seems such a stable and permanent social form that many biblical interpreters speak as though human beings must have always had equivalents of it. Ever since sedentarization and the founding of city-states—from Neolithic Jericho in the Levant to Mohenjo Daro and Harappa in the Indus Valley—there must have been nation-states. But those ancient city-states were, in fact, face-to-face communities. Two significant step-level changes were required before the nation-state emerged. To understand the New Testament, the political-social interaction that emerged with ancient city empires, from Assyria onward, is most significant. I consider each briefly (for these perspectives I am indebted to James). Table 5 offers a comparative set of traits for these modes of political-social interaction.

FACE-TO-FACE	FACE-TO-GRACE	FACE-TO-MACE	FACT-TO-SPACE
• Paterfamilias	• Patron-client	• Followership	• Democratic state
• Patriarchal family, generalized reciprocity	• Patronage, reciprocal loyalty of clientship, birth-ascribed authority	• Followership of near peers (counts, bishops, etc.), office-based ascribed authority	• Democratic rights and obligations, office-based on acquired authority
• Person-to-person contact	• Broker extended contact	• Agency-extended contact	• Disembodied-extended contact
• Direct contact with authority	• Direct contact with broker, then with authority	• Indirect contact with authority	• No contact with authority
• Wandering and/or fixed place	• Fixed places connected by overlapping networks of personal agents	• Fixed places connected by overlapping networks of bureaucratic agents (clerics)	• Mobile populations connected by overlapping networks of information
• People see each other as fellow kin, fellow village mates	• People see each other as fellow ethnics	• People see each other as fellow subjects	• People see each other as fellow citizens
• People associate with authority by copresence	• People associate with authority by personal representatives or personal agents	• People associate with authority by personal institutional representatives or bureaucrats	• People associate with authority by impersonal institutional representatives or bureaucrats
• Interaction: reciprocal, continuous, with concrete others	• Interaction: reciprocal, sporadic, with concrete patron	• Interaction: centrist, sporadic, with representatives	• Interaction: centrist, sporadic, with impersonal bureaucrats
• Space is coterminous with extended kingroups; shaped like a single centripetal circle	• Space is coterminous with ethnic groupings; shaped like contiguous centripetal circles	• Space is coterminous with controlled groups; shaped like a Tinkertoy configuration	• Space is territorial, clearly marked off and controlled; shaped by boundaries on a landmass
• Patria means birthplace; space is people inhabiting space	• Patria means birthplace; space is people inhabiting space; bureaucracy is *familia* of reigning king	• Patria is kingdom ruled by monarchy; space is group occupied; bureaucracy is servant class of kingdom	• Patria is territory of the national state; space is territory; bureaucracy is civil service of state
• Language is vehicle of magic; truth language and power language	• Language is vehicle of revelation; sacred language and civilizing language	• Language is vehicle of unique truth with ontological qualities; sacred language not to be translated	• Language is pragmatic tool of low context society

(Table 5 continued on next page)

FACE-TO-FACE	FACE-TO-GRACE	FACE-TO-MACE	FACT-TO-SPACE
• Polity coterminous with kin-groups and ancestors	• Polity forms imperium of various ethnic groups in vertical form, with various sacred/cosmic centers	• Polity forms single centripetal and hierarchical structure, cosmically central	• Polity is heterogenous, boundary oriented, and horizontal
• Adherents of the polity are kin	• Adherents of the polity are the civilized	• Adherents of the polity are the saved	• Adherents of the polity are fortunate citizens
• Legitimacy of kin-group (polity) derives from divinity	• Legitimacy of king derives from divinity	• Legitimacy of monarchy derives from divinity	• Legitimacy of government derives from the governed
• Polity defined by birth processes	• Polity defined by center and centripetal relations	• State defined by center and porous boundaries	• State defined by demarcated territory
• Information: face-to-face memory	• Information: aural writing; read aloud by personal representatives	• Information: aural writings; read aloud by official representatives	• Information: ocular writing—disembodied communication
• Copresence: individuals are engulfed and supported by the physical presence of others	• Copresence: individuals are engulfed and supported by the physical presence of others	• Copresence: individuals are engulfed and supported by the physical presence of others	• No presence: copresence is chosen, with no one to support, much less engulf others
• Tradition rooted in shared memory engulfs and supports the group	• Tradition in written form— interpreted by ethnic group specialists—supports the group	• Tradition in written form—interpreted by officials—supports the group	• Traditions self-consciously maintained and selectively culled
• Time rooted in nature and organic processes	• Time rooted in nature and calendrical in shape, determined by group specialists	• Time rooted in social forms (bells, sundial) to guide daily organic rhythms, plus calendars determined by officials	• Time rooted in social forms (clocks, watches) and prescinding from daily organic rhythms
• Space determined by kin-group's origin and location	• Space determined by ethnic group's origin and location plus greater connecting network	• Space rooted in allegiances to and territories of controlling monarch (or bishop, Pope, sultan)	• Space is territorial affiliation and allegiance chosen by the individual

TABLE 5
Four Modes of Political-Social Interaction

1. Face-to-Face Modes of Social Interaction

Face-to-face integration maintains the continuing association of persons predominantly by co-presence. Social integration is rooted in directly embodied and/or particularized mutuality of persons in social contact. Tribal society has this level as its sole form. The limitations and possibilities of interaction are defined by the modalities of co-presence, reciprocity, continuity, and concrete otherness. Kinship based on the existential significance of being born of a particular body into lines of extended blood relation is a key social form of face-to-face integration. A person remains bound by blood or affinity even after death, hence ancestrism is a significant feature of such groups.

This mode of integration is not "natural." As a matter of fact, it has to be learned and attended to after it has disappeared as the central organizing principle of a group. For example, James notes that the proverb: "Blood is thicker than water" dates only to the early seventeenth century. The demand for national unity based on "blood and soil," as articulated by societies that emphasize a myth of ethnic purity, arises only long after the ontological setting of being bound by kinship and locale has been qualitatively reconstituted. The need to reconstitute "blood and soil" as the basis for nation building indicates how radically this mode of integration has changed.

Instances of face-to-face interaction are constitutively different when set in the context of subsequent, radically different levels of integration. They are different today from what they were in the past. For example, in spite of Zionist "Bible games" and Christian fundamentalist biblical warrants, the present occupiers of Palestine are strong in ideology but quite weak in their understanding of the biblical promises of land and seed forever. To begin with, the land cannot be owned in a face-to-face arrangement; rather, it supports tribes and is owned by God. And second, centrally focused seed or blood relations require patriarchy and a patriarch. Democracy in the modern nation-state is diametrically opposed to "blood and soil" ideologies. But totalitarianism, even in the form of Israel's "ethnic purity," requires some form of "blood and soil" ideology.

2. Face-to-Grace Modes of Social Interaction

Broker-extended integration maintains the continuing association of persons with those in control of their well-being through interpersonal relations with those who can mediate with sources of power. Those in control exercise their authority by means of a bureaucracy consisting of personal representatives, often slaves, who form the imperial or elite household (for the household of Caesar, see Weaver 1972). The representatives of the emperor themselves, being household members, really have no power on their own; they have no forces at their command. Yet they can be effective on behalf of others because of their influence and inducement abilities. Imperial bureaucrats interact with geographically separated groups by means of local elites, themselves often personally (face-to-face) connected to the emperor (such as Herod the Great). Just as merchants selling identical wares were grouped together in the same quarter of the ancient city yet were not in competition, so too with brokers. There really were no competitive networks of brokers; instead there were brokers with varied clientele, with different specializations, with access to different sources of power along a vertical continuum (see Wallace-Hadrill 1990).

Ancient empires, from Assyrian to Roman, were personal bureaucratic empires with their bureaucracies personally accountable to the emperors. Thanks to Hellenism, the Roman Empire conceived of its Greek-speaking adherents as civilized, as constituting the central occupants of the inhabited world, the *oikoumene*. They communicated through the medium of a civilized and civilizing language (Greek), linking various ethnic communities to a cosmopolitan order of power. Yet this classical ecumenical community linked by civilizing language had a character distinct from the imagined communities of modern nations. One crucial difference is that English (once French) is not the language of civilization, but of economics. Furthermore, Roman confidence in the civilizing quality of Greek influenced Roman ideas about admission to membership in their *oikoumene*. Romans looked with approval on barbarians who painfully learned Hellenistic (rather than Roman) ways. People grouped in ethnic entities eventually considered each other part of a common *oikoumene*, the inhabited "household" world under the patronage of the emperor of all, and thus one of his epithets was *pater patriae* (father-patron of the fatherland). Roman expansion by conquest brought civilization in its wake. While insisting on fitting recompense for their efforts, Roman ideologues believed their purpose was to civilize all the inhabitants of the *oikoumene*, not to simply conquer them.

Roman conquest entailed requisite extortion in tribute and taxation. To call such conquest and its aftermath "oppression" is anachronistic. "Oppressed" people are oppressed essentially because they are denied their rights. But no one in the period knew he or she had "rights," legal, human, or otherwise. There was the respect due to certain persons by custom (for example, to honor father and mother), but to call this a right is to switch cultural perspectives. It is important to note that in the first-century Mediterranean "materialism was not deeply ingrained in the culture" (Humphreys 1993: xx). To accept goods and services in exchange for civilization would be considered quite fair. Goods could be material and nonmaterial and reciprocity would follow regardless of the physical or nonphysical nature of the goods in question. It was later in the Medieval period that simony (the buying and selling of church office) became a problem; it was not so for early Jesus group members who believed in a material recompense for preaching, for teaching, and perhaps for healing (for example, 1 Tim 5:18; a tradition found already in Matt 10:10 [food for teaching]; Luke 10:7 [wages for teaching]). Similarly, Romans would in no way think it "exploitation" to accept material goods and services in exchange for civilization.

Moreover, it was Hellenism that the Romans believed they were to propagate, not Roman power (see Veyne 1989: 385–415). The contiguous centripetal circles of ethnic groups in the *oikoumene* were replicated in the ethnic enclaves of various *poleis* after the model of the catholic empire envisioned by Alexander. *Patria* is still a person's birthplace, the *pater* still has supreme control over the kin-group. Yet, at face-to-grace level, the *pater* extends to one's patron as well, and the *patria* covers the birthplace of all who would seek patronage. It was the *pater patriae*, the supreme patron of the fatherland, who deserved supreme honor (the title of August, Cicero and others; see Elliott 1990a: 176).

Hellenistic peoples of the empire believed in the nonarbitrariness of the spoken sign. The signs were considered emanations of higher reality, not randomly fabricated representations of it. Think of "Alpha and Omega" as summing up the nature of God in Revelation, or the fact that the "name" of a being signified its essential reality. In effect, ontological reality is best understood through a single, privileged system of representation: the civilizing language of Greek, the language of Greco-

Roman Hellenism. As the civilizing language it was imbued with an impulse largely foreign to nationalism. There was, in fact, no nationalism in ancient empires. There were ethnic groups defined and determined by place of birth and nurture and sky overhead, but no nations (see Malina and Neyrey 1996). To live in the *oikoumene* was to be civilized, and the civilizing language of Greek encapsulated the impulse towards conversion. Conversion in the Hellenistic and Roman worlds did not mean the acceptance of particular religious tenets. It meant a sort of resocialization through the gateway of the culture shock that comes with being engulfed in a culture different from one's native experience. A Hellenistic person would consider it a sort of alchemic absorption into the life of the *oikoumene*. The barbarian becomes "Greek," that is, Hellenized. The whole nature of a person's being is malleable.

The Old Testament was translated, hence translatable, into the civilized language of Greek; it was as civilizable as persons who spoke Hebrew, Aramaic, or any other Semitic language. The New Testament, in turn, was written in the civilizing language itself, in Greek. For Jesus Messianists, the Word of God, the sacred speech, was the person Jesus, not the New Testament documents. Within Jesus groups, all languages were equidistant (and thus interchangeable) signs for the world, quite separate from the personal Word of God (apart from Alpha and Omega and the various untranslated Aramaic utterances: *Maran atha, talitha qumi, Amen, Abba, Alleluia*).

Discreet social entities consisted of ethnic groups located in the land of their birth, covered by a segment of the sky that impacted on group members and influenced ethnic traits. Group boundaries were determined by the presence of group members in a given landscape. For people in this context, elite "lords" were the only imaginable form of social control. To be "lord" meant to have total control of persons, animals, and things in one's domain. This was right and proper. Of course the lords themselves were controlled by local kings, themselves controlled by the Roman emperor. This was not so much a vertical hierarchy as it was a sequence of precedence laid out horizontally in centripetal fashion over the *oikoumene*.

Face-to-grace control had only aural writing. The technology of writing expands memory techniques, but even written documents had to be read aloud. The authority of the document depends on the authority of the reader. Official documents were read by personal representatives of the emperor or king, while documents of revelation were directed to prophets and royal personages alone. Thus Luke 10:23-24 states: "How honored are the eyes which see what you see! For I tell you that many prophets and kings desired to see what you see and did not see it, and to hear what you hear, and did not hear it" (see Hanson 1996 for this translation). Matthew 13:17 changes this to: "many prophets and righteous persons," i.e., members of Matthew's community. Sacred documents were to be read and interpreted by personal representatives of the deity (for example, 2 Kgs 22–23, Neh 8:1-11; and see Festugière 1950: 336–54). In Israel these include kings and priests (Matt 2:3-4; Mark 12:24//Matt 22:29) and prophets such as Jesus and Paul.

The prevailing interactive mode throughout the *oikoumene* was patronage and patron-client relations (see Malina 1988; Moxnes 1991).

3. Face-to-Mace Modes of Social Interaction

With European feudalism, agency-extended relations between the controlled and the controller emerge. Agency-extended integration maintains the continuing association of persons predominantly by means of representatives of institutions. An agent here is a person who acts on behalf of a person with an institutionalized social role. This is acting as legal representative, as a legally empowered middleman or medium. Agency, the process of exerting power or being in action on behalf of another, is exercised on behalf of an institution, such as the political religion or the government.

Networks of agency-extension overlapped and were often in competition. The bishop's agents might conflict with the local lord or monarch's agents. An abstract political concept of space was created at this stage. Such abstract space prescinded from persons who occupied space and gave it its social identity. For example, Israel ceased to be the people occupying a given land, but became the land itself. Thus the social identity of space is transformed into real estate. As previously noted, at the face-to-face level, *patria* is a person's birthplace (*pater* has supreme control); at agency-extended level, *patria* is the kingdom, the *communis patria*; persons could now kill their very own *pater* for the *patria*. At the face-to-grace level, the bureaucracy consists of the monarch's servants, his *familia*; at the agency-extended level the bureaucracy moves more to the role of servants of the kingdom or state, regardless of the monarch. In Western Christendom—an agency-extended creation—the bureaucracy consists of servants of the church, with the Pope himself now called "servant of the servants of God," servant of the bureaucrats who support him.

Western Christendom as it emerged in feudalism while centered in Rome, the Islamic empire centered in Baghdad, and the Byzantine empire centered in Constantinople are instances of agency-extended integration levels. Western Christendom with its Roman Pontiff in control even of the Holy Roman Emperor constituted a cosmically central entity through the medium of a sacred language (Latin) linked in a superterrestrial order of power. Islam with its sacred Arabic and Byzantium with its Greek felt quite the same. Yet such sacral communities linked by sacred languages had a character distinct from the imagined communities of modern nations. One crucial difference was the older communities' confidence in the unique sacredness of their languages, and thus their ideas about admission to membership. In effect, ontological reality is apprehensible only through a single, privileged system of representation: the "truth-language" of Church Latin, or Qur'anic Arabic, or Byzantine Scriptures and Greek Writings of the Fathers (similarly Mandarin Examination Chinese). As truth languages imbued with an impulse foreign to nationalism, these languages embodied the impulse towards conversion. As mentioned previously, conversion was not so much the acceptance of particular religious tenets, it was total absorption into a way of life: Catholic, Islamic, or Byzantine. The barbarian unbeliever becomes Christian or Muslim. The whole nature of a person's being is sacrally malleable. The sacred scriptures must be preserved in their sacred languages, the languages of the prevailing institutions (see Anderson 1991: 36).

Furthermore, the fundamental conceptions about social groups were centripetal and hierarchical. *Oikoumene* (empirewide "household") yields to *ekklesia* (worldwide Christendom), or *umma* (worldwide Islamic community of faith). The astonishing power of the Pope in Christendom (and *mutatis mutandis* of the emperor in Byzantium or of the caliph in Islam) is only comprehensible in terms of a trans-European, international, literate, clerical order and a conception of the world, shared by virtually everyone, that the bilingual intelligentsia, by mediating between vernacular and Latin (or Greek or Arabic), mediated between earth and heaven. The awesomeness of papal excommunication (or imperial or caliphate condemnation) reflects this cosmology.

While patrimonial authority (extended kinship, reciprocal loyalty) and patronage continued unabated, there were new face-to-face modalities. At the level of controlling authority, the newest form was "followership." "Followership" here means the highly personal, face-to-face bonding between a chief or central personage and his retinue of near peers. A monarch followership would include locally based agents (*comites* or counts over a "county"), circulating agents (*missi dominici*), and extended family members serving as bishops or as abbots. From about 800 to 1300 C.E., feudal followership was interpreted as though it existed from Roman times.

The distinctive form of authority at the agency-extended level was legal authority. Legal authority is ascribed authority, authority conferred on a person because of the office he (or she, for example, abbesses) held. In the feudal era there was confusion between person-based and office-based authority, usually in favor of traditional face-to-face values. People eventually believed they owned and were their office. The person was now sacred because he (rarely she) embodied a sacred agency.

Agency-extended integration required the possibility of storing and transmitting information across time and space in a way that stretched the capacities of personal or word-of-mouth memory. Writing here was an embodied medium of extension. It was basic to the stabilization of the varied forms of centrally administered agency extension. Writing continued to be spoken—extemporaneous or prepared writing, therefore personalized and concrete utterance—contextualized by the presence of a speaker, the embodied presence of some extended agency for social interaction and integration.

Writing stays aural throughout this stage. It becomes ocular, a disembodied medium of extension, only at the next level of integration. Ocular writing, disembodied writing, required a series of separations. Printing would separate speaker from document (fifteenth century); the telegraph separated sender from message (nineteenth century); while ocular writing coupled with low levels of literacy would separate high-status and low-status languages (twentieth century). Thus Anderson observes:

> Essentially, I have been arguing that the very possibility of imagining that nation only arose historically when, and where, three fundamental cultural conceptions, all of great antiquity, lost their axiomatic grip on men's minds. The first of these was the idea that a particular script-language offered privileged access to ontological truth, precisely because it was an inseparable part of that truth. It was this idea that called into being the great transcontinental sodalities of Christendom, the Ummah Islam, and the Mandarin test. Second was the belief

that society was naturally organized around and under high centers—monarchs who were persons apart from other human beings and who ruled by some form of cosmological (divine) dispensation. Human loyalties were necessarily hierarchical and centripetal because the ruler, like the sacred script, was a mode of access to being and inherent in it. Third was a conception of temporality in which cosmology and history were indistinguishable, the origins of the world and of men essentially identical. Combined, these ideas rooted human lives firmly in the very nature of things, giving certain meaning to the everyday fatalities of existence (above all death, loss, and servitude) and offering, in various ways, redemption from them. The slow, uneven decline of these interlinked certainties first in Western Europe, later elsewhere, under the impact of economic change, "discoveries" (social and scientific), and the development of increasingly rapid communications, drive a harsh wedge between cosmology and history. No surprise then that the search was on, so to speak, for a new way of linking fraternity, power and time meaningfully together. Nothing perhaps more precipitated this search, nor made it more fruitful, than print-capitalism which made it possible for rapidly growing numbers of people to think about themselves, and to relate themselves to others, in profoundly new ways. (Anderson 1991: 36)

4. Face-to-Space Modes of Social Interaction

Disembodied-extended integration maintains the integration of persons by means of networks of connections where modalities of face-to-face interaction, clientelism, and the continuing practices of intermediate agents are not salient features of political control and social relation. In disembodied-extended political social interaction, humans as bodily beings are discounted by technologies of communication and exchange across time and space, the "information society." This mode of social interaction emerges only with the nation-state.

The nation-state has its roots in the dawning humanism of the Renaissance period. At that time a number of persons sensed that the events of classical history and legend as well as those of the Bible were not separated from the present simply by a span of time. Instead, completely different conditions of life existed in the past. The subsequent discovery of new lands made it possible for Europeans to think of Europe as only one among many civilizations, not necessarily the chosen or the best. Finally, out of multiple experiences and experiments in the Americas, Europeans learned to think in terms of the following imagined realities: nation-states, republican institutions, common citizenships, popular sovereignty, national flags and anthems, and so on. Thinking in terms of these categories entailed the liquidation of their conceptual opposites: dynastic empires, monarchical institutions, absolutisms, subjecthoods, inherited nobilities, serfdoms, walled ghettoes, and so forth.

Furthermore, the validity and generalizability of the American experience (South America as well as North America) as blueprint were undoubtedly confirmed by the plurality of the independent states that soon arose. In effect, by the second decade of the nineteenth century, if not earlier, a model of the independent national state was available for adoption by human groups around the world (Anderson 1991: 37–65).

Media at this level do not rely on the prior face-to-face relationship of sender and audience (newspapers, television, radio, Internet). Yet they assume ontological continuity of the embodied office holder and the disembodied sets of images that make the office holder present to the governed. The nation-state thus consists of distant, privatized, and/or still localized strangers integrated by media as disembodied-extended linkage, providing new immediacy. We are there with a new nationalism at the Olympics, World Cup Finals, the Gulf War, and the United States-inspired NATO war in the former Yugoslavia. People speak and act in the name of the nation while effectively acting to displace it.

The experience of change, that is, time, is made even more abstract. When it comes to tradition, features to be handed down have to be chosen by individuals rather than experienced as engulfing and supporting them. Tradition is now a self-consciously maintained, selected set of practices. And human bodily presence is rendered equally abstract. Physical co-presence has to be chosen by individuals, rather than engulfing and supporting them. Co-presence is a self-consciously maintained, selected set of persons with whom one might wish to interact, often passively (while watching television programs, listening to the news, speaking on the phone).

Finally, space too is now abstract. Space is not the land of one's birth and nurture, but rather a territory marked off and controlled by some central power. Allegiance to such territory can be and often is chosen by individuals. Territorial affiliation must be self-consciously maintained.

5. Summary of The Four Modes

James concludes that modern nations only become possible within a social formation constituted in the emerging dominance of relations of disembodied extension. With each new level of integration, the previous level is reconstituted in terms of the dominance of the more abstract level, and yet the new level is viewed as equally "concrete" as the previous one. These levels of social relations are part of the reconstitution of the form of one's circle of everyday associations: with fellow kin, fellow ethnics, fellow subjects, fellow citizens. They do not occur on the same plane of development, but mark step-level, even ontological, changes. Previous levels of ontological being are emptied at the intersection of the old and the new level.

Antiquity:
Face-to-Face and Face-to-Grace Perspectives

Perhaps the easiest access to the face-to-face and face-to-grace perspectives of antiquity is to draw a sharp picture of the present main mode of social interaction rooted in the recent phenomenon of the nation-state. The nation-state is about 250 years old, rooted in the Enlightenment and the various revolutions of the eighteenth century. Nations are imagined communities. Anderson notes: "In fact, all communities larger than primordial villages of face-to-face contact (and perhaps even these) are imagined. Communities are to be distinguished not by their falsity/genuineness, but by the style in which they are imagined" (1991:6).

Nation-states are imagined in terms of clear "national" boundaries, well-marked in the soil as one crosses national boundaries as well as on maps, as any atlas clearly illustrates. Anderson aptly observes:

> These days it is perhaps difficult to put oneself empathetically into a world in which the dynastic realm appeared for most men as the only imaginable "political" system. For in fundamental ways "serious" monarchy lies transverse to all modern conceptions of political life. Kingship organizes everything around a high center. Its legitimacy derives from divinity, not from populations, who, after all, are subjects, not citizens. In the modern conception, state sovereignty is fully, flatly, and evenly operative over each square centimeter of a legally demarcated territory. But in the older imagining, where states were

Face-to-Face
- Economics embedded in kinship = face-to-face interaction normal (barter).

- Religion embedded in kinship = face-to-face interaction normal. Religious behavior like customary barter. God(s) related to as kin members; ancestrism normal.

Face-to-Grace
- Economics embedded in politics = face-to-grace or broker-extended interaction normal (government controlled political economy and agglomeration of taxes) with secondary economics (barter) embedded in kinship = face-to-face interaction secondary.

- Religion embedded in politics = face-to-grace or broker-extended interaction normal; religious behavior is government controlled at central political temples.

- Power, political and politico-religious, is retrieved from sources thanks to mediation of brokers/mediators: priests, prophets, freelancers. Structures can be precarious. There is a secondary religion, however, embedded in kinship = hence face-to-face interaction secondary, often replicating face-to-grace structures, for example, home altar, private temple, favorite broker, etc. God(s) related to as sources of power through brokers; ancestrism normal.

Face-to-Mace
- Economics embedded in politics = face-to-mace or agency extended interaction normal (government controlled political economy with centristic use of resources through taxation; resources used to maintain institutional hierarchy) with secondary economics (barter) embedded in kinship = hence face-to-face interaction secondary.

- Religion embedded in politics = face-to-mace or agency extended interaction normal; religious behavior is institutionalized within government structure.

- Power, political and politico-religious, derives from God through agents of secondary religion embedded in kinship = hence face-to-face interaction secondary. Previous private replications of face-to-grace structures now institutionalized as part replications of hierarchical structures, for example, home shrines, patron saints, favorite priests, etc. God(s) related to as royalty with agents; ancestrism normal.

Face-to-Space
- Economics disembedded and free standing = face-to-space or disembodied-extended interaction normal (the market) with secondary economics embedded in kinship (barter) as well as embedded in politics (government controlled economy) = hence face-to-face and face-to-mace interaction secondary.

- Religion disembedded and free standing = face-to-space or disembodied-extended interaction normal. Religious behavior results from "need" forces (like market forces in economics). With secondary religion embedded in kinship as well as embedded in politics (civil religion) = hence face-to-face and face-to-mace interaction secondary. God(s) related to as disembodied force; group embedded God(s) and equally available, but quaint.

TABLE 6

Embedded Economics and Embedded Religion
with Modes of Political Interaction

defined by centers, borders were porous and indistinct, and sover-
eignties faded imperceptibly into one another. Hence, paradoxically
enough, the ease with which pre-modern empires and kingdoms were
able to sustain their rule over immensely heterogeneous, and often
not even contiguous, populations for long periods of time. (1991: 19)

Social geographers define territoriality as "the attempt by an individual or group to affect, influence, or control people, phenomena, and
relationships, by delimiting and asserting control over a geographic
area" (Sack 1986: 19). Further: "Territoriality for humans is a powerful geographic strategy to control people and things by controlling
area. . . . Territoriality is a primary geographical expression of social
power. It is the means by which space and society are interrelated. Territoriality's changing functions help us to understand the historical relationship between society, space, and time" (ibid.:5). In the face-to-grace
oikoumene of the Romans, territoriality is like a water-filled sponge in
which each ethnic group, like each bubble in a sponge, maintains its own
shape while sharing the same water, the water of Romanized Hellenism.
In face-to-mace situations, the geographic area is more like ripples ema-
nating from a center, with ever lower and disappearing outward wavelets
marking off the end of central influence. It is only with face-to-space
abstract nation-states that territoriality embraces a clearly marked off
geographic area, with a governmental claim to sovereign rights over the
area and with travelers required to have passports!

Any considerate reading of the New Testament requires empathetic
assessment of the modes of interaction in face-to-face and face-to-grace
societies. Social groups at the time were always ethnically centripetal,
arranged in terms of precedence in the *oikoumene*. They were focused on
central personages, such as a father in the patriarchal family or local
ruler in a kingdom or emperor in the empire. Social structure was concerned with power, hence premised on vertical dimensions. There were
no landed, territorial boundaries to mark off any social unit. While
farmland had boundary stones, those who farmed the land lived
together in villages, where they were bound together in face-to-face living as village-mates, often kin. There were also common lands available
to village livestock, but there were no village or town boundaries, and
certainly no kingdom or national boundaries. (For a comparative model
of "territory," see Sack 1986: 71.) Lands were known by their inhabitants.
For example, the land of Israel did not mean the land called Israel, but

the land where an ethnic group of persons called Israel lived. Note that both Egyptian and Akkadian used different determinatives for kingdoms and ethnic groups. It would seem that modern maps of biblical lands are really ethnocentric, not unlike the maps of Africa and the Middle East drawn up by nation-states in the colonial period. For example, note the bewilderment among Arabs about the United States' recent insistence on boundaries between Kuwait and Iraq! As for biblical maps, perhaps instead of boundaries marking off Samaria, Galilee, and other areas with lines, maps ought only have blobs of color indicating the claimed ethnic affiliation of the population in given areas.

DEALING WITH RELIGION
BEFORE NATION-STATES

Before the rise of nation-states with their characteristic and presumed separation of church and state, religion must have been part of the state, otherwise how could it be separated from it? Before the emergence of the nation-state, religion—embedded in politics and kinship—accounted for the contingency and ineluctability of a human existence. It was the ancestral God or gods, or the God or gods of the city, who directly or indirectly controlled a person's particular genetic heritage, gender, life era, physical capabilities, mother tongue, and so forth. These kinship and political deities offered comfort in face of human suffering: disease, mutilation, grief, age, death. Thanks to the deity's control of fertility, human mortality was transformed into continuity since continuity was symboled in kinship, with offspring indicating connectedness, fortuity, and fatality.

With the Enlightenment and the dusk of Christendom, some thinkers adopted a model of continued progress and change. Such a model entails intimations of step-level changes and positive growth that supercede what preceded. Such thinking was hostile to continuity. But now nation-states come to offer the continuity that religion previously provided. They develop the perception of an immemorial national unity, ancient history, and provable existence as a nation. Note, for example, how modern Ashkenazi Jews, largely deriving from eighth century C.E. Khazar converts to the Talmudic Jewish religion, insist that Abraham, Isaac, Jacob, as well as the ancient kings and prophets of Israel, were all "Jews"—presumably following the Mishnah and Talmudic regulations. "France (and every nation-state) is eternal." Nation-states "always loom

out of an immemorial past, and, still more important, glide into a limit-
less future. It is the magic of nationalism to turn chance into destiny"
(Anderson 1991: 9).

Rᴇʟɪɢɪᴏɴ ᴀɴᴅ ᴛʜᴇ Mᴏᴅᴇs
ᴏꜰ Pᴏʟɪᴛɪᴄᴀʟ Sᴏᴄɪᴀʟ Iɴᴛᴇʀᴀᴄᴛɪᴏɴ

In societies or segments of societies in which social integration is
effected largely through face-to-grace interaction, religion is embedded
in kinship and politics. The result is that kinship norms, forms, and values configure domestic religious behavior of the kinship (for example, in
households and spheres of concern to the kin-group). But political
norms, forms, and values configure religious behavior of the political,
public kind (for example, temple worship, sacrifice, publicly required
rituals for coronation, agriculture, warfare, calendar, and spheres of concern to the public and its authorities).

First-century embedded religion had domestic religion and ritual as
well as political religion and ritual. Political religion saw to the well-
being of the city or town: temples with stone altars on which to sacrifice
animals (as well as vegetables and minerals); hence temples smelling of
burnt meat with blood, gore, heaps of animal skins; priests to hack up
animals; festival days and games marked by a god's presence, multiple
deities, divine emperors and equally heroic ancestors, and so on. Then
there were the stories of the gods and their public benefaction; these stories were publicly proclaimed and sung at festivals or other occasions.
People also knew of specialized temples for healing, for divination, for
specific devotions to cover distinctive aspects of life. What distinguished
ancient political religions was that there was no all-purpose religion (just
like there was no all-purpose money in the political economy). Domestic religion, on the other hand, looked to the well-being of the household. Ancestors, protective nonvisible persons (genii, demons, spirits),
household gods, and family stories figured prominently (see MacMullen
1981 and Malina 1996a for extensive examples).

Face-to-mace political religion took the shape of the political institution: rigidly institutionalized in hierarchical mold and made visible in
the monarchic state. Whether headed by the Pope and the person he
appointed and controlled as emperor and king in the West, or headed by
the Byzantine emperor and those he appointed and controlled as eccle-
siastical patriarchs and bishops in the East, the fixed hierarchy made vis-

ible the divine hierarchy, headed by the single and sole God who rules the cosmos so providentially. The topmost person was the agent of God, while those elites below the topmost person were agents of their superiors. Pope Innocent III (1198–1216) could say at his inaugural: "I am the Vicar of Jesus Christ, the successor of Peter, and I am placed between God and man, less than God, but greater than man: I judge all men, but I can be judged by none" (cited by Charles 1913: 22). This is an appropriation of the face-to-grace concept of the person of the monarch: "The king is the last of the gods as a whole, but the first of human beings" (*Corpus Hermeticum* Vol. III Fragment XXIV, 3rd ed., Nock and Festugière, 53). Thus in the West the Pope was the agent of God, "the vicar of Christ on earth," the bishops were the agents of the Pope, priests were agents of their bishops—like that other divine appointee, the king, with his followership. Papal ritual is replicated in the court ritual that replicates church ritual. An international clerical corps ran the bureaucracy of the political church and of the religious state. The faithful made pilgrimages to sacred power sites, just as the clerical estate moved in its own pilgrimage to the state power sites. And along with this political religion, there was kinship religion to deal with domestic affairs: guardian angels, patron saints, home altars, endless folk practices (still to be witnessed in Mediterranean Christianity, see Sweeney 1984).

Finally, face-to-space social interaction spawned a separation of previously embedded religion from its political moorings. Consequently, a historical understanding of Mediterranean-based religions before the eighteenth century requires a model of substantive religion. Such a model implies that if religious behavior is "embedded" in patterns of life that are not primarily religious, religious conduct will be dominated by criteria other than purely religious ones. In other words, the operative categories will not be those of the sociology of religion: formal religion with its theology as orthodox or modernistic; liturgy as simple or high church; denominational organization as church, sect, or cult; clergy as monastic or secular; piety as incarnational or eschatological; ethics as systematic or situational; and world view as gloomy or hopeful. These categories, of course, befit post-Enlightenment disembedded religion.

To summarize, the total social fabric during the time of Jesus consisted of politics and kinship. The formulations of an enveloping, overarching, generalized order of existence were rooted in symbols interwoven in those specific social institutions that supported the broader goals of society, that is, in kinship forms and political forms. In other words, "supernatural" beings will be members of kin or political units and treated in terms of those institutions rather than in terms of some free-standing, discreet, religious institution separated from kin and polity, from family and state. There would be no pretensions at universal religion until there would be a universal political institution (such as Justinian's Christendom) or universal kinship group (such as the Stoic brotherhood of males and the fatherhood of Zeus).

Religion and First-Century Mediterranean Face-to-Grace Social Interaction

In societies or segments of societies where social integration is effected largely through face-to-grace interaction, religion is distinctively embedded in politics. Political norms, forms, and values configure religious behavior. Yet face-to-grace forms exist together with the previously prevailing face-to-face forms and their kinship-embedded religions. For example, in a face-to-face perspective, the creation of the cosmos is procreation (not in the Bible) or fabrication (like a potter or a gardener, as in Gen 2:4b-24). With the coming of face-to-grace social integration and political religion, the creation of the cosmos is a ruler's command ("Let there be . . ." as in Gen 1:3-27). Both perspectives exist side by side. This was the situation during the time of the New Testament.

The embedded religion typical of face-to-grace social interaction was political religion. It would be readily apparent to Greeks, Romans, and Israelites that Jesus groups really had no real religion like ethnic groups usually did. After all, Jesus groups were not ethnic groups characterized by geniture and geography, as all ethnic groups were. Face-to-grace political religions were real, public religions. Political religions could be seen, smelled, touched, and heard because there were temples, sacrifices, priests to slaughter animals, ritual symbols, ritual objects, and daily observances at the temple.

The scenario most befitting the story of Jesus is one of politically embedded religion. Jesus proclaims his message, describes his task, and directs his symbolic actions at the pillars of politically embedded Israelite Yahwism. To proclaim the kingdom of God with God's rule imminent is clearly a political statement in which religion is embedded, as is talk of who is near or far from the kingdom, of what the kingdom of God is like, of praying to God for God's kingdom to come, of kingly judgment, and kingly reward and punishment—all these represent political language for a first-century person. Jesus taught in public, the arena of politics, and came to Jerusalem to proclaim his prophetic message at the very center of political religion, the temple. The political powers of that center—priests, council, and prefect—had him killed on the political pretext of his supposed claim to being "king of the Judeans," a group of people whose king had been removed by Rome for incompetence and replaced by a Roman prefect. While Jesus presented a prophetic proclamation concerning a forthcoming political overhauling of Israel's political religion (the rule of God), Jesus' death in Jerusalem put the plan in abeyance. The followers of Jesus believed God raised Jesus from the dead so that Jesus himself would soon emerge as the vice-regent of Israel's God, as Israel's Messiah with power.

Athenian tetradrachma from the Hellenistic period; the head of the
helmeted Athena Parthenos (obverse); an owl standing on an amphora
and the names of the mintmasters, surrounded by an olive branch
(reverse); Staatliche Museen, Berlin

ᘓ 4 ᘏ

THE KINGDOM
AND POLITICAL ECONOMY

If the kingdom of God proclaimed
by Jesus was a theocracy, a political institution with religion and
economics embedded, then the kingdom clearly had an economic
dimension. Many modern Christians seek to take their moral cues for
daily living from the Bible. The words and examples presented in New
Testament books are seen to offer direct religious sustenance for
twenty-first-century people intent upon pleasing God. Such twenty-
first-century people find themselves in a world often assessed in terms of
Gross National Product, where quantity orientation—judging one's own
success in terms of numbers—is a normal occurrence. Human worth
often hangs in the balance with countable money: the cost of a quality
education, of necessary hospital surgery, of a house and clothing that
match one's status, and of job searches emphasizing income rather than
satisfaction. When persons from this background read the New Testament, the rescue they often seek from God is in terms of the right
amount of money at the right time for their own purposes. After all, the
Lord exalts those of low degree, fills the hungry with good things, and
sends the rich away empty (Luke 1:51-52). On the other hand, there are
well-to-do people who consider themselves "good Christians," yet would
have their fellows believe they are serving God not mammon (Matt 6:24;
Luke 16:13), and who would never give a thought to selling all they have
and giving it to the poor (Mark 10:21; Matt 19:21; Luke 18:22). The issue
of rich and poor is often resolved in the minds of pious wealthy Christians
by the belief that the poor are poor because they are lazy or unfortunate or

both. The poor know that the rich are rich because they have had "the breaks." Fortunately, most Americans still belong to a middle class, and the New Testament has no words for the middle class. Why?

The purpose of this chapter is to consider what the political economy of the kingdom of God might entail. There is every reason to believe that in the eastern Mediterranean in New Testament times, "rich" or "wealthy" as a rule meant "avaricious, greedy people," while "poor" referred to persons scarcely able to maintain their honor or dignity. Thus the words are not opposites and really refer to two qualitatively different spheres. Secondarily, in nonmoral contexts, the wealthy were contrasted with the needy in terms of access and control of the necessities of life that were available to everyone. The moral problem was the essential wickedness of the wealthy who chose to serve greed rather than God. The story of the Greedy Young Man pointed to how easy that could be (Matt 19:13-22). For a camel could pass through a tiny needle's eye far easier than the greedy rich (Matt 10:25). On the other hand, the defenseless and weak are declared honorable, for theirs is access to God's forthcoming kingdom. Why this translation?

LINGUISTIC COLLOCATION

A first step in interpreting the meaning of "poor" and "rich" or "wealthy" would be to consider the lexical company that the words keep. This is called their linguistic collocation. The words in question are used alone or in the company of other words that might clarify their ranges of meanings. For example, from passages in which the word "poor" is used without further description, we simply cannot get any idea of what the authors are referring to except by sticking our own ideas into their words (for example, Matt 19:21; 26:9-11; Mark 10:21; 14:5, 7; Luke 18:22; John 12:5-8; 13:29; Rom 15:26; 2 Cor 6:10; 8:9; 9:9; Gal 2:10). The same holds for the word "rich" (for example, Luke 14:12; 16:1; Eph 2:4; Rev 2:9; 13:16).

On the other hand, there is also a series of passages in which the word poor is used in the company of other words that describe the condition of the person who is labeled poor. Thus, Luke 4:18 has a quote from Isaiah in which the poor are classed with the imprisoned, blind, debt-ridden. Matt 5:3, along with Luke 6:20-21, ranks the poor with those who hunger, thirst, and mourn. Matt 11:4-5 lists the blind, lame, lepers, deaf, and the dead with the poor; while Luke 14:13, 21 has the maimed, lame, and the blind. Further, Mark 12:42-43 and Luke 21:2-3 speak of a poor widow, and Luke 16:20-22 tells of the poor Lazarus who was hungry and full of sores, hence ill. Finally James 2:3-6 points out the shabbily dressed poor man as truly powerless; while Rev 3:17 considers the poor to be wretched, pitiable, blind, naked—categories similar to the list in Matt 25:34-46, where we find the hungry, thirsty, stranger, naked, and imprisoned (but not poor!). These adjacent descriptions of the poor point to the poor person as one who has undergone some unfortunate personal history or circumstance.

Within these collocations, the poor rank among those who cannot maintain their inherited status due to circumstances that befall them and their family, such as debt, being in a foreign land, sickness, death (widow), or some personal physical accident. Consequently, the poor would not be a permanent social class, but a sort of revolving class of people who unfortunately cannot maintain their inherited status. And day laborers, landless peasants, and beggars born into such situations are not poor for economic reasons. Anyone who worked for a daily wage was considered poor and needy by minority, wealthy elites (for example, Philo, *Spec. Laws* 4:195-96), mainly because of the precariousness of such a person's social position.

As for the wealthy, there is likewise a series of passages in which the word "rich" or equivalents are used with other words, giving indication of the quality of the rich condition. Thus in Mark 12:41-44//Luke 21:1-4: rich people control an abundance of resources from which they can give large sums, and are contrasted with a poor widow. The rich are presumed by nonelites to have ready access to God (Mark 10:23-24//Matt 19:23-24//Luke 18:23-25) since they do in fact have ready access to the human powers that be, for example, Joseph of Arimathea (Matt 27:57). In Luke 1:53 "rich" is the opposite of "hungry" and parallel with "mighty, proud"; similarly Luke 6:24-25: the rich are already consoled; they are among those who are full now. Luke 12:16 speaks of a rich man in a context of covetousness and greed: "Take heed, and beware of all covetousness; for a man's life does not consist in the abundance of his possessions" (v. 15 RSV); this person "is not rich toward God," but lays up treasure for himself—he is greedy (v. 21). Thus Luke accuses the Pharisees of greed ("lovers of money" 16:14 RSV) in a context about serving God or greed. Further, in Luke 16:19-31, a rich, well-satisfied man with a large family of brothers is contrasted with the poor, suffering, ill, and family-less Lazarus. Finally, Luke 19:1-10 tells of the rich Zacchaeus who as chief tax collector takes from the poor and defrauds.

Then, 1 Tim 6:10 points to greed as the root of all social evils. The author notes that the rich in this world are haughty, set their hopes on uncertain riches; instead these should be like God in being benevolent, liberal, and generous (1 Tim 6:17; 2 Tim 3:1-4 ranks avarice second after selfishness). James 1:10-11 would have the rich man face the fact he will die while in pursuit of riches, hence should act accordingly, "humbly." God's chosen, the poor, rich in faith and heirs of the kingdom, are overlooked in favor of the rich who tyrannize, rush to court, publicly shame the name "invoked over you" (James 2:6-7 RSV). Perhaps the fullest description of the moral quality of being rich is in James 5:1-7: the rich trust in their perishable possessions—in garments, gold, silver, fields, amassed goods; they keep back wages of laborers who work for them and harvest their fields, defraud them, condemn the righteous, kill the righteous. In Rev 3:17-18, the rich are those who prosper, while needing nothing; they are opposed to the wretched, pitiable, poor, blind, and naked. They rank with the kings of the earth, great men, generals, and the strong (Rev 6:15). Those presently growing rich are the merchants (*emporoi*), those with ships at sea (Rev 18:3, 15, 19).

Now if we take all these adjacent descriptions of the rich and group them in terms of what they have in common, it would seem that they became rich as the result of their own covetousness or greed or that of their ancestors. Amassing of surplus, having more than enough and more than others is typical of the rich. Significantly, one was presumed to have become rich by depriving others; defrauding and eliminating others; prospering by having others become wretched, pitiable, ill, blind, and naked. Thus the rich rank with persons who wield power for their own aggrandizement, such as kings and generals, or with the haughty and others who overstep their proper social rank, such as merchants (see Malina 1993: 90-112).

On a morally neutral level, as seen frequently in the Wisdom books, the rich and poor simply mark the extremes of the social body in terms of elite and nonelite status. But in a moral context, rich meant powerful due to greed, avarice, and exploitation, while poor meant weak due to inability to maintain one's inherited social station. Consequently, the opposite of rich would not necessarily be poor. In the perception of people in peasant society, the majority of people are neither rich nor poor; rather all are equal in that each has a status to maintain in some honorable way. "The Lord makes poor and makes rich" (1 Sam 2:7 RSV). Personal value is not economic, but a matter of lineage. In this context rich and poor characterize two poles of society, two minority poles—the one based on the ability to maintain elite status, the other based on the inability to maintain one's inherited status of any rank. Why this range of meanings?

As previously mentioned, words realize meanings from social systems. For example, to understand the meaning of the word "democratic" as used by current citizens of the United States or of the People's Democratic Republic of China, it is insufficient to look at fifth-century B.C.E. democratic Athens. The polis of Athens, with its distinctive social arrangements, would provide a third set of meanings for the word along with the two modern ones based on United States and Chinese social systems, respectively. So it is that the meanings of first-century Mediterranean social systems are understood by means of words in texts from that time and place. And it is the social system that requires us to look at the greedy and the weak rather than the rich and the poor. Ancient Mediterranean ways of perceiving and judging differ markedly from our own. A comparative look at social structures as well as a consideration of some first-century stereotypes will illustrate the point.

COMPARING SOCIAL SYSTEMS

As noted in the previous chapters, biblical writings developed exclusively within the contexts of kinship and politics. They come from writers whose main concerns were with domestic religion and political religion, as well as domestic economy and political economy. Thus, biblical authors never spoke of economics purely and simply; their language was never used to express systems of meaning deriving from technology. The problem was not with their language, since speakers of modern Hebrew and Greek do quite well in articulating economic and religious theory. The point is that during the period from which the biblical writings date, the existing social systems simply did not have freestanding and formal religion and economics. The vocabulary and system of distinctions in the theology of the Bible, for example, worked within kinship and political systems. There is no developed biblical terminology descriptive of market economies or economic theories and the abstract meanings rooted in them. Therefore, economic dimensions of society have to be converted through and into belonging (wealth is meaningless unless convertible into honor) and power (for example, public office). The economic dimension of the social system has no focus in and of itself.

If all this is too abstract, consider the concrete case of the poor and the wealthy in Mediterranean village society (see Rothenberger 1978). There wealthy, "sonless" women whose husbands have died are referred to as "poor widows." In what sense are they poor? Surely not in any economic sense. Similarly, in antiquity, the label "poor" was "'applied in particular to the vast majority of the people in any city-state who, having no claim to the income of a large estate, lacked that degree of leisure and independence regarded as essential to the life of a gentleman.' . . . the poor as recipients of a wealthy man's benevolence would primarily be unfortunate members of his own class . . . some ought to be poor (Aristotle) and deserve misfortune (Cicero)" (Mullin 1984: 17; this book contains a large collection of information, often anachronistically interpreted).

If the word "poor" presently refers mainly to economics, that simply reflects our contemporary social arrangement and says nothing about any other society. To find out to what noneconomic poor might refer, we must examine the basic social structures people use to realize and express their values. Such an exercise should enable us to see that the designation poor takes on a different meaning, a meaning determined by the social structure of the culture in question. As a general rule, in both past and present societal arrangements, one or another of the basic four institutions described above maintains primacy over the others. Thus, for example:

- In the applied Marxism of North Korea or the People's Republic of China, kinship, religion, and economics are subordinate to politics—in other words, to the norms of politics. Religion and economics are determined by the political institutions: politicians of one type or another govern.
- In the United States and to a slightly lesser extent in western Europe, kinship, religion, and politics are dominated by economics—the norms of kinship, religion, and politics are determined by economics. Here persons owning and/or controlling wealth ultimately make the laws that determine the social order: the wealthy rule.
- In Latin America and in most Mediterranean countries, religion, politics, and economics are subservient to kinship, and the kinship institution determines the norms of religion, politics, and economics. Wellborn persons rooted in the "best" families control society in their role as patrons. Latin American libera-

tion theology, for example, is rooted in the practical attempt to dislodge economics from kinship and embed it in politics.

・ Finally, in modern-day Islamic republics and in medieval Christendom, kinship, economics, and politics are governed by religion. The norms of kinship, economics, and politics are determined by the political religious institution: representatives of the political religious institution rule these societies in one way or another.

What does the overriding desire for more and more goods mean in a society with the political institution in the ascendancy (greed; avarice), or with the economic institution as central (profit motive), or with a focal kinship institution (covetousness), or with the religious institution as paramount (divine blessing)? How does the meaning of the word "poor" change when used to mean the *oppressed* (the politically unable; for example, in Exodus the empowerment of the poor; during the Israelite monarchy, the consolation of the poor) the *indigent* (the economically unable), the *sick* and *outcast* (the kinship unable: those who cannot maintain their honor by themselves), and the *unbelieving*—and therefore ignorant (the religiously unable: in Islam, unbelief is ignorance)? Metaphorically speaking, all such "poor" people are marginal, but not to society in general. Rather they stand at the margins of their social group; the specific problem in understanding is the margin in question. Which of these margins are considered socially significant?

Indications of a Different View of the World

Given the model of the four basic social institutions (kinship, economics, politics, and religion), economics in Mediterranean antiquity was embedded in kinship or in polity and was not a freestanding adaptive institution. The Roman Empire structurally resembled the applied Marxism of the People's Republic of China (or the former Soviet Union), while the rest of the Mediterranean area was structurally much like Latin American rural realities of large landed tracts owned by patronal families and served by client villagers. These are embedded economies. An embedded economy means that economic goals, roles, production, hiring, firing, and planning are determined by kinship or political considerations, either alone or primarily, and not purely or primarily on the basis of economic considerations (see Hollenbach 1985; for a general overview of the development and subsequent disappearance of peasant societies and the emergence of eventual industrial forms, see Worsley 1984).

If we turn to the relevant truisms of the Mediterranean world, I suggest that three cultural norms can shed light on the discussion: all goods are limited, no one goes without necessities, and the wealthy are inherently evil. These "self-evident truths" of the New Testament period seem to indicate that if any economic themes can be mined from the broad sweep of our scriptures that might befit first-century Mediterranean scenarios of how the world works, they would be: 1) conviction of the futility of extra effort or labor; 2) the common experience that no one suffers inordinately or dies for lack of the necessities of life; and 3) the fact of the wickedness of the wealthy. All of these common biblical themes are generally out of favor today, both in fact and in theory. Most Americans believe that an extra job pays off. Further, in capitalist countries (and in the state capitalism of communism as well), people do die or suffer inordinately for lack of the necessities of life, while even the most Bible-believing churches have some very wealthy supporters who do not believe themselves vicious! The perceptions of the first-century Mediterranean world do not fit our contemporary values and experience; neither do the economics and social structures of antiquity. In other words, our experience does not serve to help us understand what biblical authors said and meant to say since biblical evaluations about rich and poor do not fit our contemporary world. Let us further consider the truisms mentioned above.

1. All Goods Are Limited

Aristotle already noted: "For the amount of such property sufficient in itself for a good life is not unlimited" (*Politics* III, 9 1256b; LCL). This means that everything of value in life can be increased only at the expense of others. The reason for this assessment is that in the first-century Mediterranean world, just as in nearly all peasant societies, all goods are believed to be limited. Foster has noted:

> broad areas of peasant behavior are patterned in such fashion as to suggest that peasants view their social, economic, and natural universes—their total environment—as one in which all of the desired things in life such as land, wealth, health, friendship and love, man-

liness and honor, respect and status, power and influence, security and safety, exist in finite quantity and are always in short supply as far as the peasant is concerned. Not only do these and all other "good things" exist in finite and limited quantity, but in addition there is no way directly within peasant power to increase the available quantities. It is as if the obvious fact of land shortage in a densely populated area applied to all other desired things: not enough to go around. "Good," like land, is seen as inherent in nature, there to be divided and redivided, if necessary, but not to be augmented. (Foster 1965: 296; see Gregory 1975)

The result is a zero-sum game in which any individual or group advancement is done to the detriment of others. This item of information from cultural anthropology serves to explain not a few perceptions and prescriptions in biblical literature. For example, "For you know the grace of our Lord Jesus Christ, that though he was rich, yet for your sake he became poor, so that by his poverty you might become rich" (2 Cor 8:9 RSV). It clarifies why the wealthy are believed to be wicked. Their control over more actual wealth than others is due to their own or their ancestors' taking advantage of others. Some authors gratuitously deny the existence of an ancient perception of limited good (see Foster 1972). However, these authors cannot explain the institutionalized envy, hence the Mediterranean "evil eye," typical of the culture. References to the evil eye occur in the Old Testament in these instances: Deut 15:9; 28:54, 56; Prov 23:6; 28:22; Sir 14:3, 6, 8, 9, 10; 31:13; 37:11; Tob 4:7, 16. In the New Testament, even Jesus refers to this social reality more than once: Matt 6:22-23; 20:1-15; Mark 7:22; Luke 11:34-36; Gal 3:1; 4:14 (spit, rather than despise; spitting being a common strategy for deflecting the evil eye; see Elliott 1988; 1990b; 1992; 1994a; Neyrey 1988). The Hebrew and Greek phrase "evil-eye" is usually translated as "grudge," "envy," and similar terms (Hagedorn and Neyrey 1998). The existence of this behavioral feature underscores the perception of limited good. We return to this point below.

2. No One Goes without Necessities

Whatever else it might mean, the parable of the lilies of the field (Matt 6:25-32), certainly indicates that the things necessary for human subsistence were at hand. In line with the picture in that parable, it was a truism at that time and in that cultural area that: "No person is destitute

when it comes to the necessities of life, nor is any person overlooked"
(see Clement of Alexandria, *Paidagogos*, II, 14, 5, SC; Seneca, *Epistles*
17, 9; Plutarch, *On Love of Wealth*, 523F; LCL; as well as Cicero, Muso-
nius Rufus, and others cited by Hermann Usener [1887: 339–40, par.
602]; this was the common wisdom of the period, first articulated in
the Epicurean school). The axiom obviously verifies common experience. And the exception well known in antiquity is the period when
everyone lacks basic necessities due to drought, famine, or war. At
such a time, money is of no value, as Aristotle notes: "a man well supplied with money may often be destitute of the bare necessities of
subsistence, yet it is anomalous that wealth should be of such a kind
that a man may be well supplied with it and yet die of hunger" (*Politics* III, 16 1257b; LCL). Therefore, money is not true wealth. For biblical interpretation, it is significant that such an assessment of money
is no longer common in the contemporary Western world. It is further
significant that today there are people in industrial societies who do in
fact lack the necessities of life.

3. The Rich Person Is Inherently Evil

A. INHERITED WEALTH IS STOLEN WEALTH—It seems that a common perception in the ancient Mediterranean about the wealthy was that "Every
rich man is either unjust or the heir of an unjust person"; while another
version had it that "Every rich person is a thief or the heir of a thief"
("*Omnis dives aut iniquus aut heres? iniqui,*" St. Jerome, *In Hieremiam*,
II,V,2, CCL 74, p. 61; and similarly in *Tract. de Ps* LXXXIII, lines 29–30,
CCL 78, p. 96; *Epistle* 120: to Hedebia, PL 22, p. 984: "*Dives autem iniquus
aut iniqui haeres*" (A rich person however is a wicked person or the heir of
a wicked person) cited as the commonly held viewpoint "*vulgata senten-
tia*" (popular opinion). This assessment can be easily traced back in time
in the area, both among elites such as Plato, *Laws*, 12, par. 743, LCL: "The
very rich are not good," and among nonelites: Menander has a character
call the rich "burglars" (frag. 129 K), and notes elsewhere that "no one
gets rich quickly if he is honest" (frag. 294 K), (Allinson 1921: 346, 386),
and see the commentary on these verses in *The Dyskolos of Menander*
(Handley 1965: 21); note also: "A visible friend is a better thing by far than
wealth which you keep buried out of sight," and the commentary on this
axiom on pp. 273–74). That every rich person is a thief or the heir of a
thief was a truism based upon perception of limited good. If all goods are

limited, and people were created more or less on equal footing, then those who have more must have taken it from those who now have less—or their ancestors did. Hence ancestors were wicked for having stolen, while the heirs are wicked for harboring stolen wealth. There were no deserving rich. Given limited good, it was quite normal to be envious of the wealthy. Of course, as Philo notes in his comments on Deut 30:5, all this will one day change: "all the prosperity of their fathers and ancestors will seem a tiny fragment, so lavish will be the abundant riches in their possession, which flowing from the gracious bounties of God as from a perennial fountain will bring to each individually and to all in common a deep stream of wealth leaving no room for envy" (*On Rewards and Punishments* 168).

B. THE AMASSING OF WEALTH RESULTS FROM AVARICE—Wealth is meant to meet the needs of human living. It is to be used with contentment and satisfaction. Consequently, wealth is meant simply as another means for acquiring and maintaining honor. When the acquisition of wealth is an end, not a means, then the person dedicated to wealth acquisition is inherently demented, vicious, evil. Not a few of the ancients remark on this aspect of human experience. Pseudo-Pelagius, presumably circa 400, remarked: "For persons to cease to be greedy, they must cease to be wealthy" (*On Wealth* II; PLSup I 1381), or again: "It is scarcely possible for a rich person to keep from committing crimes" (XX, 4; PLSup I 1417).

In other words, the rich might be presumed to be wicked on the basis of a series of commonly held, stereotypical assessments. Gallagher (1982) marshals a range of cultural cues that controlled perception among second-century Mediterraneans and thus facilitated anti-introspective judgments: that genealogy can be deduced from one's subsequent behavior and character (and behavior/character offer solid indication of one's genealogy); that social standing necessarily determines one's abilities or lack of them (and ability or inability is clear proof of one's social standing); that a person who does something for all humanity is of divine birth (and divine birth points to benefits for all humanity); that kings necessarily perform valuable actions of benefit to many (hence actions that benefit many point to some royal agent). Further, magic is effective only among the ignorant and immoral; the ignorant and immoral are addicted to magic; magicians are fearsome, threatening, and suspicious persons; hence fearsome, threatening, and suspicious persons are almost certainly magicians. Good and honest persons are preoccupied with continuity and antiquity—they respect the past; those who advocate a break with the past, who advocate something brand new, are rebellious, outsiders, and deviants. And, our case in point, if a person is wealthy, he or she is wicked or an heir of wicked people.

Plutarch, certainly a well-situated person by any economic standards, did not consider himself "wealthy." Rather he mocked the wealthy and dissociated himself and his coterie from that group because of their need for ostentation ("they consider wealth as non-wealth and a blind alley and a dead end unless it has witnesses and spectators as a tragedy. But the rest of us (*hemin*) . . ." (*Table Talk* V, 5 679 A-C; LCL). In the treatise *On Love of Wealth* (LCL) he comments at length on the wealthy, noting the following stereotypical characteristics of that category of people:

1. They put everything away under lock and seal or lay it out with moneylenders and agents; thus wealthy persons go on amassing and pursuing new wealth, wrangling their servants, farmers and debtors (525A; 17).

2. The wealthy are either avaricious or prodigal. The greedy miser feels compelled to acquire more and more, yet is forbidden to enjoy the acquisitions: miserly, unsocial, selfish, heedless of friends, indifferent to civic demands, and yet the avaricious suffer hardships, lose sleep, engage in traffic, chase after legacies, truckle to others (525C; 19). Thus the greedy rich: kill and destroy men without using what they destroy; take from others what they cannot use themselves; what they pass on to their heirs is their avarice and meanness, a warped character and no formation in basic humanity (526BC; 25).

3. The heirs of the greedy rich "catch the taint of avarice directly from their fathers," they assimilate their father's life, steal before their father is dead, then upon death, become transformed persons: "There is instead interrogation of servants, inspection of ledgers, the casting up of accounts with steward and debtors, and occupation and worry that deny him his luncheon and drive him to the bath at night" (526EF; 27–29). Thus, avaricious, wealthy fathers take away leisure and freedom from their heirs, offering overwhelming and overpowering wealth.

4. The prodigal or profligate rich person, on the other hand, is a legal blackmailer, pursuer of legacies, cheats and carries on intrigues, schemes, has a network of likeminded friends— but puts wealth to no use. But prodigals call a truce to their

acquisitiveness once they are affluent and well provided for (525F; 23). While they too kill and destroy men as they accumulate wealth, yet unlike the greedy, they use what they destroy (and so are better than the miserly).

5. In between the greedy and the profligate rich are those politically well-situated, who accumulate vast amounts of wealth for political utility: "Let kings and royal stewards and those who would be foremost in their cities and hold office engage in money-getting." These are motivated by ambition (love of honor), pretension, and vain glory and need the wealth to give banquets, bestow favors, pay court, send presents, support armies, and buy gladiators (525D; 21).

What characterizes all the wealthy is their lack of contentment, of satisfaction—and this at the expense of others. Even apart from New Testament voices, such evaluations of the rich are not rare in the time and area, notably from people labeled Stoics and Cynics. Such generalizations can help the modern interpreter see what his/her first-century counterpart may have seen because of how they stereotypically saw. One thing they saw was the necessary wickedness of the wealthy. For this reason, it is not adequate to say that the biblical texts witness recognition of the dangers of wealth, as modern theology might have it (for example, in the recent pastoral letter of the Roman Catholic Bishops: *Economic Justice for All* par. 51). The texts reveal a pervasive conviction of the wickedness of the wealthy (for example, further mirrored in the Council of Carthage in 401: "All the emperors must be requested, because of the affliction of the poor (*pauperes*) with whose suffering the church is enervated without intermission, that they delegate for them defenders against the power of the wealthy (*diuites*) with the supervision of the bishops" (CCL CCLIX 202).

THE PURPOSE OF WEALTH

True wealth, that deriving ultimately from the domestic economy as Aristotle noted, was meant to maintain human beings in a sufficiently contented way of life. People were to be satisfied with having their needs met, even in noble style. This was *autarkeia* (see 2 Cor 9:8; Phil 4:11; 1 Tim 6:6; the independence of 1 Thess 4:12). As a rule, anyone could meet this goal, as Jesus presumes in the parable of Matt 6:25-32 and as Stoics and Cynics alike insisted. Wealth was simply another means for acquiring and maintaining honor. But due to the hoarding and avarice of the wealthy, the poor were deprived of the honor due them. This is an especially acute problem for Jesus and his proclamation of the restoration of Israel. The Priestly reformers responsible for Leviticus 25 sought to alter the process by which the majority of Israelites were reduced to the shame of poverty while their better-placed "neighbors" amassed their lands and offspring. Jubilee every fifty years allowed every Israelite "to return to his property and . . . return to his family" (Lev 25:10). Thus ancestral lands were to be returned and families were to be restored on that land. Further, the jubilee year was a Sabbath year (as in Jesus' proclamation in Luke 4:17-21; Lev 25:11-12). As Philo noted, jubilee meant restoring "the prosperity of the past" to the present (*Spec. Laws* 2, 122; LCL). Given the perception of limited good and an embedded economy, Jesus' injunction to give one's goods to the poor is not about self-impoverishment, but about redistribution of wealth; and motives for giving to the poor are not rooted in self-satisfying charity, but in God-ordained, socially required restitution.

With the rise of Jesus groups outside of Palestine, the problem is no longer restitution and redistribution of wealth in Israel, but the "conversion" of the wicked wealthy. Here the wealthy are to share their goods with their fellow Jesus group members. This easily fit into Hellenistic common sense. As Plutarch remarked, the felicity of wealth is to parade one's possessions as in a theater, before spectators and witnesses: "With no one to see or look on, wealth becomes lackluster indeed and bereft of radiance" (*On Love of Wealth*, 528A; LCL). But greed was out. Even for the Hellenist, the wealth derived from trading, interest taking, and any other form rooted in acquiring money for the use of money was essentially suspicious, if not downright perverted. Such wealth is an end, not a means to the good life (see Aristotle, *Politics* III, 12-20 1257a-1258a; LCL). The pursuit, acquisition, and maintenance of such wealth is inherently demented, vicious, and evil—witness the wealthy.

In summary, adequate reflection on New Testament scenarios peopled by the wealthy and the poor requires attention to the social system of the time and place. That social system had its focus on kinship and politics; it shared the perception of limited good and urged contentment with readily available necessities of life. Cultural criteria of the day had the word "poor" pointing to the socially impotent and bereft, while the labels "rich" or "wealthy" were attached to the greedy and avaricious.

I suggest that if any economic themes can be mined from the broad sweep of scripture that might befit first-century Mediterranean scenarios of how the world works, they would be: 1) the wickedness of the wealthy; and 2) the common observation that no one dies or suffers inordinately for lack of the necessities of life. However, it would seem these perceptions do not fit our experience in the United States; neither do the political economies and social structures of antiquity. Our experience does not help us to understand what a biblical author said and meant to say.

The themes of "poverty" and "the poor" in an economic sense were not focal in New Testament times or in the New Testament. Instead, the proclamation of the kingdom of God with God controlling his own land in terms of Torah jubilee entailed the redistribution of wealth in Israel and restitution on the part of the wealthy Israelites. Such redistribution and restitution as part of the political economy willed by God were of primary concern, as in the Torah and the Prophets. Here is where the wickedness of the rich fits in. Furthermore, concern for the economic destitution of "the little people" is a modern construct since, by all accounts, the poor had enough for the necessities of life. While Jesus group members in regions with largely Israelite populations may have consisted of the destitute (*ptochoi*), and while those in communities where Israelites were a minority mainly consisted of poor day laborers and smallholders (*penetes*, "little people," Stegemann 1984: 55), these are assessments true in terms of nineteenth-century industrial revolution categories. What would they mean in the first century?

In the first-century Mediterranean world, the only freestanding social institutions were politics and kinship. Poverty refers to the inadequacy of life without honor with the consequent social and personal inability to participate in the activities of the community, the inability to maintain self-respect as defined by community social standards. If goods are used to alleviate or eradicate such inadequacy, would goods be "to have," "to use," or "to mean"—and in what proportion, to what end, and how? Given the fact that economics was an embedded institution coupled with the perception of limited good, Jesus' injunction to his fellow Israelites to give their goods to the poor is not about self-impoverishment, but about redistribution of wealth. With the advent of the kingdom of God, motives for giving to Israel's poor were not rooted in self-satisfying charity, but in God-ordained, socially required restitution. This is how persons got their affairs in order (repentance) in preparation for God's taking over the country.

Via Dolorosa, Jerusalem, the West Bank

❧ 5 ❧

The Kingdom and Jesus' Self-Denying Followers

To assist him in the task of proclaiming the kingdom of God, the traditions related in early Jesus group documents mention that Jesus recruited a faction. What he required of faction members was "to follow" him. This following required self-denial. Over the past two millennia, the themes of following Christ and self-denial have undergone a wide range of transformations and appropriations so that the original meaning of these behaviors has been lost. In this chapter I consider self-denial in the following of Jesus. The Synoptic passages that transmit this theme are those statements about self-denial in Mark 8:34//Matt 16:24//Luke 9:23. This set in the triple tradition is embedded in the context of Jesus' first announcement of his forthcoming death in Jerusalem, the first of three such announcements. The saying on self-denial comes as a climax to a previous saying about Jesus' death, as follows.

> From that time Jesus began to show his disciples that he must go to Jerusalem and suffer many things from the elders and chief priests and scribes, and be killed, and on the third day be raised. And Peter took him and began to rebuke him, saying, "God forbid, Lord! This shall never happen to you." But he turned and said to Peter, "Get behind me, Satan! You are a hindrance to me; for you are not on the side of God, but of men."

> Then Jesus told his disciples, "If any man would come after me, let him deny himself and take up his cross and follow me. (v. 24)

For whoever would save his life will lose it, and whoever loses his life for my sake will find it. For what will it profit a man, if he gains the whole world and forfeits his life? Or what shall a man give in return for his life?" (Matt 16:21-26)

∽

And he began to teach them that the Son of man must suffer many things, and be rejected by the elders and the chief priests and the scribes, and be killed, and after three days rise again. And he said this plainly. And Peter took him, and began to rebuke him. But turning and seeing his disciples, he rebuked Peter, and said, "Get behind me, Satan! For you are not on the side of God, but of men."

And he called to him the multitude with his disciples, and said to them, "If any man would come after me, let him deny himself and take up his cross and follow me. (v. 34)

For whoever would save his life will lose it; and whoever loses his life for my sake and the gospel's will save it. For what does it profit a man, to gain the whole world and forfeit his life? For what can a man give in return for his life?" (Mark 8:31-37)

∽

But he charged and commanded them to tell this to no one, saying, "The Son of man must suffer many things, and be rejected by the elders and chief priests and scribes, and be killed, and on the third day be raised."

And he said to all, "If any man would come after me, let him deny himself and take up his cross daily and follow me. (v. 23)

For whoever would save his life will lose it; and whoever loses his life for my sake, he will save it. For what does it profit a man if he gains the whole world and loses or forfeits himself?" (Luke 9:21-24)

In the statement in question, the pattern is A/B/B'/A': follow—self-denial—cross-bearing—follow. Clearly, self-denial is parallel to taking up the cross. Now there is another tradition about taking up the cross that makes no reference to self-denial. Instead of reference to self-denial, there is emphasis on family denial. This is the Q tradition, also included in the *Gospel of Thomas*.

> Do not think that I have come to bring peace on earth; I have not come to bring peace, but a sword. For I have come to set a man against his father, and a daughter against her mother, and a daughter-in-law against her mother-in-law; and a man's foes will be those of his own household. He who loves father or mother more than me is not worthy of me; and he who loves son or daughter more than me is not worthy of me; and he who does not take his cross and follow me is not worthy of me. (Matt 10:34-38 RSV)

ⳗ

> Now great multitudes accompanied him; and he turned and said to them, "If any one comes to me and does not hate his own father and mother and wife and children and brothers and sisters, yes, and even his own life, he cannot be my disciple. Whoever does not bear his own cross and come after me, cannot be my disciple." (Luke 14:25-27 RSV)

ⳗ

> Jesus said: He who does not hate his father and his mother will not be able to be my disciple (*mathetēs*), and (he who does not) hate his brothers and his sisters and (does not) bear his cross (*stauros*) as I, will not be worthy (*axios*) of me. (*GThom* 55)

ⳗ

> <Jesus said:> He who does not hate his fa[ther] and his mother as I (do), will not be able to be my [disciple (*mathetēs*)]. And he who does [not] love his [father and] his mother as I (do) will not be able to be my [disciple (*mathetēs*)], for (*gar*) my mother <gave me falsehood> but (*de*) my [true mother] gave me life. (*GThom* 101)

Since renouncing one's kin-group is parallel to taking up the cross, it would seem from this saying that such renunciation is also much like self-denial. Further, kin-denial and self-denial would both be equivalent to taking up the cross to follow Jesus. The collocation of this set, then, is very suggestive.

Many commentators pose the question of the source of these sayings (for example, Bultmann 1963; Langkammer 1977 and their references). The Q and *Thomas* sayings would clearly antedate the Synoptic gospels. And it would seem the block in Mark likewise antedates that gospel document since it is a compilation of disparate elements (Bultmann 1963) that cluster as part of the threefold announcement of Jesus' death. Such a threefold pattern is typical of oral lore. However does any of the tradition derive from Jesus? That the triple tradition and Q/*Thomas* are pre-Synoptic suggests some reworking in those hidden halls of traditioning, but in what direction? Some commentators call upon that one other passage in the Synoptics that likewise enjoins "taking up." This other tradition, according to which Jesus asks people to equivalently take up something, not the cross, is that in M (material unique to Matthew), dealing with what Jesus styles as "my yoke" (Langkammer 1977: 215): "Come to me, all who labor and are heavily laden, and I will give you rest. Take my yoke upon you, and learn from me; for I am gentle and lowly in heart, and you will find rest for your souls. For my yoke is easy, and my burden is light" (Matt 11:29-30 RSV). There is a parallel of sorts to the first part of this statement in the *Gospel of Thomas*: "Jesus said: Come to me, for my yoke is benign (*chrestos*) and my rule is gentle; and you will find rest (*anaupasis* [sic]) for yourselves" (*GThom* 90).

Since the *GThom* passages lack any reference to "taking up" the yoke, the M saying about taking up the yoke is quite distinctive. The general consensus is that this M tradition is an Israelite Wisdom saying; "yoke" refers to behavior based upon distinctive Torah interpretation (see Suggs 1970: 99–108; Bultmann 1963: 159; both cite Sir 24:19-22; 51:23-26; Prov 1:20-33; 8:1-36 as illustrative). To bear Wisdom's yoke meant to keep to its ways of living out God's directives, to the Torah interpretation of Wisdom circles. To bear Jesus' yoke would mean, then, to keep to his way of living the Torah. The "easy" yoke is not one that is accommodating. It is instead one that does not lead along misdirected pathways, but truly and directly leads to the goal of the Torah (Suggs 1970: 108).

To summarize, the primary data that serve as indicators of some original saying of Jesus in this tradition would include the triple tradition saying, the Q/*Thomas* saying, and the M saying. How might we proceed to discover some original element(s) this regard? I base my suggestions on that famous principle of Bultmann's: "Conjectures are easy enough" (1963: 161, n. 2).

First, the fact that Jesus was actually crucified, and that this datum was now applied to those bent on becoming members of the Jesus Messiah group, would indicate that mention of the cross was a later development of the tradition (although Langkammer 1977: 215 thinks it is an OT reference to the Tau sign, as for example, Ezek 9:4, 6). Thus the feature of "taking up your cross" would be secondary. Likewise, it seems that reference to a yoke seems more idiomatic of Israelite custom rather than a pan-Mediterranean reference. The injunction to take up the yoke would make as little general sense as that other famous M passage in which Jesus enjoins his apostles: "Go nowhere except to the lost sheep of the house of Israel" (Matt 10:5).

Similarly, the mention of "becoming a disciple" also seems subsequent to Jesus' career as political faction founder. There is no evidence that Jesus taught a new and distinctive way of life. This would emerge in Jesus Messiah groups or Resurrected Jesus groups (see Malina 1999). Since Jesus was a political faction founder, and the earliest traditions telling of how Jesus founded his faction consist of repeated "follow me" injunctions without discipleship, the quality of the relationship of faction members to Jesus would not originally have been that of disciple to teacher. Initially, what Jesus' faction members were to do was assist Jesus in proclaiming the gospel of the kingdom and healing and exorcising with a view to the kingdom (as for example, in Matt 10:5-15).

In the present forms of the tradition, the content of taking up the cross is defined by the preceding, parallel clause: to deny self in the triple tradition and to leave family in the Q/*Thomas* tradition. As I will indicate, there is really very little difference between the two. However, since the traditions about Jesus' statements are invariably pictures or imaginable scenarios, I would choose the description of the range of family members to be hated as original. So some original tradition would have run: "If any man would come after me, let him hate father and mother [and other kin] and take up my yoke and follow me."

First in a context such as Matt 10:36-37, with the rhythm of three "is not worthy," a wisdom *mashal* in a 2 + 1 form would run as follows:

> He who does not hate father or mother is not worthy of me; and he who does not hate son or daughter is not worthy of me; and he who does not take up my yoke and follow me is not worthy of me (after Matt 10:36-37).

Or in a context such as Matt 11:28-30 coupled with Luke 14:26-27:

> Come to me all who labor and are heavy laden, and I will give you rest. Take my yoke upon you, and learn from me; for I am gentle and lowly in heart, and you will find rest for your souls. For my yoke is easy, and my burden is light.
>
> If any one comes to me and does not hate his own father and mother and wife and children and brothers and sisters, yes, and even his own life, he cannot follow me. If anyone comes to me and does not take up my yoke, he cannot follow me (after Luke 14:26-27).

The point is that in the process of traditioning, the yoke falls out and the cross is put in. What the statements represent are norms for Jesus group members recruited by Jesus to assist in his task. With the substitution of cross for yoke, the saying takes on a broader scope both in terms of audience and task. The audience now is anyone wishing to join a Jesus group, the task is living a way of life. Yoke, bearing Jesus' interpretation of the Torah for the sake of the kingdom, was confined to Israel and the Torah. It undoubtedly belonged to the same stratum as the M saying: "Go nowhere except to the lost sheep of the house of Israel" (after Matt 10:5).

In any event, it must have been a significant saying of Jesus for the practical life of later Jesus Messiah group members since it specified the conditions of following Jesus. This subsequently was called discipleship, the Jesus group way of life, that is, living in his way. What further underscores its significance is that it was reinterpreted early on, and this rather uniformly (unlike the saying on no divorce, for example, which has multiple interpretations).

The saying on taking up one's cross pointed to being ready to be shamed, to face shame, to be shamed even to death. The motivation for bearing such shame was for the sake of Jesus and the gospel, for the sake of professing the crucified Jesus. This reference to the cross and the motivation specified have wider scope. Shame fits into all the nooks and crannies of life. Following the Torah fits so many precepts or specific segments of life. Take up your cross thus generalizes a far more specific injunction or directive. Yet it surely fills out the meaning of Jesus' yoke by drawing the yoke's implications in terms of Jesus' actual fate.

In other words, while the yoke better fits a political context in the house of Israel, the cross could be adopted for fictive kin-groups and generally amplified by Mediterranean experience, wherever Romans crucified. Yet in its newly appropriated fashion, it still related to Jesus' distinctive political yoke. Regardless of whatever historical development is postulated, why would leaving the kin-group and/or taking up the cross be parallel to self-denial? What in fact is self-denial? To understand self-denial it is necessary to describe and define what is the self (as for asceticism in general, see Malina 1994b). Here I intend to develop such a description and definition in the comparative way typical of social science criticism of the New Testament (see Elliott 1993).

CULTURE-BASED TYPES OF SELF

Descriptions of human behavior follow the paths of societal structures. Just as a computer has a disk operating system, so human groups have social structures that serve as humankind's operating systems. What makes the human system work at all, the electricity so to speak, is self-interest. And the goals—both proximate and ultimate—that social structures enable are values. There is a close relationship among values, self-interests, and structures. Self-interests are proper to single persons in individualistic cultures, while in collectivistic societies, self-interests are proper to ingroups.

The subject of the entire operating system is human beings in society; that is, persons in groups, individuals in environments, and selves in relations. Persons in society are studied sociologically, individuals in environments are studied biologically, and selves in relations are studied psychologically (Harris 1989). This section deals with self/person in societal relations—the object of that fusion of perspectives called social psychology. Social psychology "is about the mesh between the self and society" (Gamson 1992: 53). The self here is defined as all the statements a person makes that include the words "I," "me," "mine," and "myself." This definition means that all aspects of social motivation are included in the self. Attitudes (I like . . .), beliefs (X has attribute Y in my view), intentions (I plan to do . . .), norms (my ingroup expects me to do . . .), roles (my ingroup expects people who hold this position to do . . .), and values (I feel that . . . is very important), are all aspects of the self.

The self is coterminous with the body in individualist cultures and in some of the collectivist cultures. It can be related, however, to a group the way a hand is related to the person whose hand it is. The latter conception is found in collectivist cultures, where the self overlaps with a group, such as family or tribe (Triandis 1989: 77–78). For the philosophical underpinnings of this enterprise, see Harré (1980; 1984; 1989). Here we have the help of social psychologists who have been working on descriptions of the self, both specifically and generally, for the past thirty years or so. The work of Harry Triandis and his colleagues is most significant. It is on the basis of Triandis's masterful overview of research that I have developed the following contrasting descriptions of the individualistic self and the collectivistic self.

In their ongoing investigation into social psychological types as matrices for culture, Triandis and others have settled upon a continuum that runs from individualistic to collectivist. Roughly speaking, individualism means that individual goals precede group goals. Collectivistic means that group goals naturally precede individual goals. With a view to comparison, I begin with a brief sketch of the individualistic notion of self prevalent in the United States and then move on to a description of the collectivistic self. The features laid out in sequence include the defining attributes of each cultural emphasis, the culture's virtues and other characteristic features, their socialization modes, self conceptions, modes of social perception, advantages and disadvantages (all in etic, comparative perspective).

THE INDIVIDUALISTIC SELF
AND SELF-RELIANCE

Individualism may be described as the belief that persons are each and singly an end in themselves and as such ought to realize their "self" and cultivate their own judgment, notwithstanding the push of pervasive social pressures in the direction of conformity. In individualist cultures most people's social behavior is largely determined by personal goals that may overlap only slightly with the goals of collectives such as the family, the work group, the tribe, political allies, coreligionists, fellow countrymen, and the state. When a conflict arises between personal and group goals, it is considered acceptable for the individual to place personal goals ahead of collective goals. Thus individualism gives priority to the goals of single persons rather than to group goals. What enables this sort of priority is focus on self-reliance in the sense of independence, separation from others, and personal competence.

For individualists in the United States, freedom and self-reliance are important values, yet they are not the defining attributes of individualism. The defining attributes of individualism are: distance from ingroups, emotional detachment, and competition. Individualists, then, evidence much emotional detachment from others, extreme lack of attention to the views of others, relatively little concern for family and relatives, and tendency toward achievement through competition with other individualists.

Individuals do what makes sense and provides satisfaction rather than what must be done as dictated by groups, authorities, parents. While guilt might be triggered by abandoning the dictates of groups, authorities, and parents, the individual is above those dictates. The cardinal virtues of individualists include: self-reliance, bravery, creativity, solitude, frugality, achievement orientation, competitiveness, concern for human rights, pragmatism, freedom, competence, satisfaction, ambition, courage; and goals such as freedom and personal accomplishment. Success depends upon ability; the outcome of success is achievement.

Other characteristics include: sexual activity for personal satisfaction (rather than procreation), future orientation (but in terms of a short time perspective), emphasis on balanced reciprocity (that is, equal exchange), use of wealth to change social structures, instrumental mastery (a need to dominate people, things such as the environment and events), exclusion of persons who are too different. Moreover, there is nearly exclusive emphasis on the nuclear family, with ready geographic mobility, the use of line dance forms rather than circle dance forms, a presumption of self-reliance and independence. Stress is placed on individual rights and individual privacy.

Consequently, socialization in individualistic cultures looks to what the person can do—to skills—and only secondarily to developing a sense of group identity. Children learn independence first. In mother-child relationships, enjoyment and mutual satisfaction (having fun together) are what count. Individualist socialization results in high scores in self-other differentiation. After parents, peer socialization is common, with a concomitant development of skills in dealing with peers (not with superiors or subordinates). Individualists may never acquire skills to facilitate the functioning of a group.

Furthermore, in individualist societies, the individual's sense of insecurity is accompanied by large expenses for police and prisons. This feature is replicated by the national sense of insecurity resulting in large military expenditures. Such cultures also display prejudice toward racial and religious groups that are too different, and demonstrate unrealistic interpersonal relationships (and unrealistic international relationships), with the significant presence of crime against persons (for example, sexual crimes, assault), more hospital admissions, and more drug abuse.

The self in individualist cultures is a bundle of personal attributes. Identity derives from what one has: skills, experiences, accomplishments, achievements, property. Attributes such as being logical, balanced, rational, and fair are considered important. People define themselves by what they do in society, not by their ingroup memberships. Social functions are judged to be individually acquired attributes, so individualists often find the behavior of collectivists in intergroup relations quite "irrational." Individualists are emotionally detached from their ingroups and do not always agree with ingroup policies. Furthermore, individualists are extremely introspective and highly psychologically minded. Individual behavior is presumed to be best explained by internal psychological mechanisms rather than by ingroup norms, goals, and values. Individualists perceive their ingroups as highly heterogeneous and they experience little sense of a common fate with ingroup members. For they often have large ingroups (for example, the entire United States), with norms that are loosely imposed, and with boundaries that are not sharp and clear but are highly permeable.

The social perception of individualists is dominated by what others in some ingroup of significance are doing. Individualists belong to many ingroups, each of which controls only a narrow range of behavior (for example, some receive only organizational dues). There is weak attachment to ingroups, with conformity to ingroup authorities determined by personal calculation; compliance can never be taken for granted. Language is low context; that is, the content of any communication is highly developed, spelled out in detail. In conflict, individualists side with horizontal relations (siblings, friends, equals) over vertical ones (parents, government).

Some of the themes distinctive to individualist literature in the United States include: dignity of humans, individual self-development, autonomy, privacy, the individual as the basis of society; individuals are used to analyze social phenomena: as the bases of political, economic, religious, or ethical analyses; individuals are the sole locus of knowledge (Lukes 1973). It has been demonstrated that behavioral sciences, evolutionary biology, and economic analyses in the United States are biased in favor of the scientists' own individualist culture, with little concern for broader human nature (Schwartz 1986).

The advantages of individualism include freedom to do one's own "thing," to maximize satisfaction, to achieve self-actualization, and to pursue creativity without paying the penalties of doing one's duty to the collective, of doing what the group expects, or of meeting one's group obligations. In industrialized/information cultures, independence, creativity, and self-reliance increase. But while individualists pursue exciting lives, experiencing a range of varied activities providing enjoyment and pleasure, at times such pursuit entails aggressive creativity, conformity, and insecurity.

Negative concomitants of individualism may also be identified. Interpersonal competition is often counterproductive (Rosenbaum et al., 1988) and can lead to distress and aggression (Gorney and Long 1980). Palmer (1972) finds individualism related to high competition, concern for status, and violence. People in individualist cultures often experience more conflict within their families than people in collectivist cultures (Katakis 1978). The greater emphasis on achievement in individualist cultures threatens the ego (Katakis 1976) and causes insecurity. Insecurity leads to excessive concern about national security and feeds the arms race (Hsu, 1981).

While in the contemporary world individualism can be found among the affluent, socially and geographically mobile, and more modern segments of every society, individualistic cultures as a whole have emerged only where Enlightenment values have permeated society and agriculture has become the occupation of the very few. The contemporary version of the individualistic self emerges rather late in human history. "The fundamental assumption of modernity, the thread that has run through Western civilization since the 16th century, is that the social unit of society is not the group, the guild, the tribe, the city, but the person" (Bell 1976: 16).

However, anthropological comparisons indicate that contemporary hunter-gatherer peoples likewise fall along the individualistic side of the continuum, while modern simple agriculturalists fall along the collectivistic. So Triandis postulates the stages of proto-individualism in ancient hunter-gatherer societies, collectivism in agrarian societies (presumably from sedentarization that began some nine thousand years ago), and finally neo-individualism in contemporary post-agrarian societies beginning in sixteenth century Renaissance city-states, with individualistic cultures underpinning the Industrial Revolution. The prime recrudescence of ancient individualism can be found in the neo-individualism that marks the industrialized, immigrant United States. The United States in nearly all examples—meaning immigrant, European United States—is emphatically individualistic, with all the typical traits of an exaggerated, overblown individualist culture.

In today's world, Triandis (1989: 48) observes that 70 percent of the world's population is collectivistic, while the remaining 30 percent are individualistic. Hofstede (1994) opts for 80 percent. As a matter of fact, individualism seems totally strange, esoteric, incomprehensible, and even vicious to observers from collectivistic societies. Again, as Triandis notes (1989: 50), what is most important in the United States—individualism—is of the least importance to the rest of the cultures of the world. The point of all these observations is to demonstrate that any self that we might encounter in the New Testament, whether in the Synoptic tradition or in Paul, must necessarily be a collectivistic self.

The Collectivistic Self and Family Integrity

Collectivism may be described as the belief that the groups in which a person is embedded are each and singly an end in themselves, and as such ought to realize distinctive group values notwithstanding the weight of one's personal drive in the direction of self-satisfaction. In collectivist cultures most people's social behavior is largely determined by group goals that require the pursuit of achievements that improve the position of the group. The defining attributes of collectivistic cultures are family integrity, solidarity, and keeping the primary ingroup in "good health."

The groups in which a person is embedded form ingroups in comparison with other groups, outgroups, that do not command a person's allegiance and commitment. Ingroups consist of persons that share a common fate, generally rooted in circumstances of birth and place of origin, therefore by ascription. While individualists belong to many ingroups, yet with shallow attachments to all of them, collectivists are embedded in very few ingroups but are strongly attached to them. Collectivist ingroups control a wide range of behaviors. A person's behavior toward the ingroup is consistent with what the ingroup expects, but behavior toward everyone else (strangers) is characterized by defiance of authority, competition, resentment of control, formality, rejection, arrogant dogmatism, and rejection of influence attempts that have the outgroup as a source.

Collectivist virtues put the emphasis on the views, needs, and goals of the ingroup rather than on single group members. These virtues include generalized reciprocity, obligation, duty, security, traditionalism, harmony, obedience to authority, equilibrium, always doing what is proper, cooperation, fatalism, pessimism, family centeredness, high need for affiliation, succor, abasement, nurturance, acquiescence, dependency, high superordination, and high subordination.

Other characteristic features of collectivist cultures include the following. Sexual relations are exclusively for procreation—a fulfillment of social duty. The virtues extolled by collectivist cultures are social virtues—attitudes that look to the benefits of the group—rather than individualistic virtues. Thus we find virtues such as a sense of shame, filial piety, respect for the social order, self-discipline, concern for social recognition, humility, respect for parents and elders, acceptance of one's position in life, and preserving one's public image. Anything that cements and supports interpersonal relationships is valued. The goal of life is ingroup (most often family) security and honor. The outcome of success in this enterprise is fame. Collectivist persons have many common goals with others in the group and engage in interpersonal relationships with long term perspective (such as mother-son; while the child is growing, this is generalized reciprocity). They use wealth to maintain social structure.

Social norms and obligations are defined by the ingroup rather than determined by behavior to get personal satisfaction. Persons harbor beliefs shared with the rest of the ingroup members rather than beliefs that distinguish self from ingroup. And group members put great stock on readiness to cooperate with other ingroup members. In the case of extreme collectivism, individuals do not have personal goals, attitudes, beliefs, or values but reflect only those of the ingroup. People in collectivist cultures enjoy doing what the ingroup expects (Shweder and Bourne, 1982).

Socialization patterns are keyed to developing habits of obedience, duty, sacrifice for the group, group-oriented tasks, cooperation, favoritism toward the ingroup, acceptance of ingroup authorities, nurturing, sociability, and interdependence. The outcomes of such socialization produce persons with little emotional detachment from others, with broad concerns for family, and with a tendency toward ingroup cooperation and group protectiveness. Thus persons in such collectivist cultures will do what they must as dictated by groups, authorities, and parents, rather than what brings personal satisfaction. The great temptation is to pursue some self-centered, enjoyable activities. Should persons yield to such temptation and be found out, ingroup sanctions run from shaming to expulsion. In conflict, collectivists side with vertical relationships (parents, authorities) over horizontal ones (spouses, siblings, friends). Furthermore, collectivistic cultures often evidence language that is ingroup specific (many local dialects), with people using context rather than content in conveying meanings: high context communication is prevalent.

The collectivist self is a dyadic self as opposed to an individualistic self. A dyadic self constantly requires another to know who one is. The collectivist self is a group self that often internalizes group being to such an extent that members of ingroups respond automatically as ingroup norms specify without doing any sort of utilitarian calculation. This is a sort of unquestioned attachment to the ingroup. It includes the perception that ingroup norms are universally valid (a form of ethnocentrism), automatic obedience to ingroup authorities, and willingness to fight and die for the ingroup. These characteristics are usually associated with distrust of and unwillingness to cooperate with outgroups. Often outgroups are considered a different species, to be evaluated and treated like a different kind of animate being.

Collectivist persons define self to outsiders largely by generation and geography: family, gender, age, ethnicity (nation), place of origin, and place of residence. To outgroups the self is always an aspect or a representative of the ingroup that consists of related, gendered persons who come from and live in a certain place. To ingroup members, the self is a bundle of roles, ever rooted in generation and geography. One does not readily distinguish self from social role. The performance of duties associated with roles is the path to social respect. On the other hand, social perception is greatly prismed through whom the other is—that is, to which group or groups he or she belongs.

Collectivist persons are concerned about the results of their actions on others in the ingroup. They readily share material and nonmaterial sources with group members. They are concerned about how their behavior appears to others since they believe the outcomes of their behavior should correspond with ingroup values. All ingroup members feel involved in the contributions of their fellows and share in their lives. Individuals feel strong emotional attachment to the ingroup, perceiving all group members as relatively homogeneous, with their behavior regulated by group norms, based on acceptance of group authorities with a view to ingroup harmony and achievement at the expense of outgroups.

Collectivism is associated with homogeneity of affect: if one's ingroup members are sad, one is sad; if joyful, one is joyful. Those in authority expect unquestioned acceptance of ingroup norms as well as homogeneity of norms, attitudes, and values. Interpersonal relations within the ingroup are seen as an end in themselves. There is a perception of limited good: if something good happens to an outgroup member it is bad for the ingroup because "good" is finite and resources are always in a zero-sum distribution pattern. Finally, the ingroup is responsible for the actions of its members. This has implications for intergroup relations. Specifically, in collectivism one expects solidarity in action toward other groups. Joint action is the norm. Authorities usually decide what is to be done and the public must follow without question. Good outcomes for the other group are undesirable, even when they are in no way related to one's own outcomes. Each individual is responsible for the actions of all other ingroup members and the ingroup is responsible for the actions of each individual member. For instance, ancient Israelites related to Romans in response to Roman policies toward the house of Israel as if each Roman established those policies. The Romans, in turn, interpreted the actions of individual "Judeans" (the Roman outgroup name for the house of Israel) that fit their general ideological framework as the actions of all Judeans.

All things being equal, collectivists seek to maintain harmony with humans and things, to live in harmony with the environment. They try to include those who are different and tend to be noncompetitive. With their emphasis on proper interpersonal relationships (all things being equal), they have less crime against persons (for example, sexual crimes, assault), fewer hospital admissions, and less drug abuse.

Collectivists evidence high rates of social support when unpleasant life events occur. Naroll's (1983) review of the empirical evidence suggests that positive social indicators characterize societies in which the primary group is a normative reference group that provides strong social ties, emotional warmth, and prompt punishment for deviance. The group is culturally homogeneous and includes active gossip, frequent rites, memorable myths, a plausible ideology, and badges of membership.

In the contemporary world, societies characterized by collectivistic cultures have low rates of homicide, suicide, crime, juvenile delinquency, divorce, child abuse, wife beating, and drug and alcohol abuse, and are characterized by good mental health. On the other hand, such societies are also characterized by dissatisfaction with the excessive demands of family life, by low gross national product per capita, and by poor functioning of the society in the political realm. Thus there is a trade-off between quality of private life and public life, which are kept quite separate.

Obviously, our Mediterranean ancestors in the Christian tradition were essentially collectivistic. When we read descriptions of the appropriations of New Testament injunctions in the past, my question is: Why did those people, who were equally collectivistic, appropriate those injunctions in the way they did? Where did they put their emphasis? How would their Christianity be distinctive in its own way? How would it matter in collective life?

THE PSYCHOLOGICAL FOCUS OF SELVES: IDIOCENTRIC AND ALLOCENTRIC

The previous comparison contrasts two types of cultures, the individualistic and the collectivistic. Researchers who have gathered information about these types of cultures would situate the "pure" types at opposite ends of a spectrum. The research demonstrates that people are enculturated in terms of socialization patterns that run along an axis whose extremes are totally individualistic and totally collectivistic. There seems little to indicate that first-century Mediterranean societies were anything other than collectivistic. And the situation seems to have stayed this way well into the European Renaissance period (notwithstanding the unverifiable assertions of French philosophers quoted by Perkins 1992: 245–47).

Along with the cultural setting of human socialization, Triandis (1993) has further pointed out the value of paying attention to the psychological bent of individuals within both individualistic and collectivistic cultures. For persons in all cultures reveal an individual psychological orientation that likewise ranges along a scale from idiocentric to allocentric. Idiocentric persons are, of course, self-centered, while allocentric individuals are other-centered. With this perspective, we can say that, just as in our individualistic society we have narcissistic, self-centered individualists as well as other-centered individualists, so in antiquity there were self-centered collectivists and other-centered collectivists.

The value of this further nuance is to distinguish the self as socialized due to cultural cues (individualistic and collectivistic) and the self as oriented by interpersonal, psychological experience.

DEFINED SELVES: PRIVATE, PUBLIC, INGROUP

One more perspective on the self specifically looks to the mesh between person and culture. While still in the context of the individualist and collectivist models, Triandis notes the ways individuals deal with how their selves are defined in the process of socialization and in later social experience. For a person's self is defined by a range of sources. Triandis distinguishes among the privately defined self, the publicly defined self, and the collectivistically defined or better, ingroup-defined, self. The outcomes of these processes of defining the self are as follows. First, there is a "private self" deriving from what I say about my traits, states, behaviors. Then there is a "public self" that refers to what the general group says about me. Finally, there is a "collective or ingroup self" that reflects what the ingroup says about me.

What is significant for understanding the self in terms of social psychology is the way the defined selves emerge in the contrasting cultural types. People from collectivist cultures sample and take stock of ingroup self-assessments far more than people in individualist cultures. In collectivist cultures there is a general inconsistency between private self and public self. People do not tell you what they personally think, but what you need or want to hear. This split is required by politeness and saving face. It is also a boundary maintenance device that serves to protect ingroup information. Thus people are enculturated to think one way and speak another. For the most part, getting along with others is valued above many other concerns. Saying the right thing to maintain harmony is far more important than telling the truth. People are not expected to have personal opinions, much less to voice their own opinions. It is sufficient and required to hold only those opinions that derive from social consensus. Social behavior derives from relative status where hierarchy is the essence of social order.

In individualist cultures, the public and private self converge because two inconsistent selves cause the individual to experience dissonance as well as to undergo a sort of information overload. Furthermore, in individualist cultures, the public self and the private self are influenced by the same factors. People are expected to be "honest" even if ignorant, "frank" even if brutal, and "sincere" even if stupid. Here one must think and say the same thing. Social behavior derives from individualist choices based on one's class affiliation.

To summarize the perspectives on the self that have been presented up to this point, consider Table 7.

Within prevailing individualistic or collectivistic cultures, single persons may turn out to be idiocentric or allocentric. When it comes to behavior springing from the ways in which the self is defined, however, individualists as a rule fuse private and public selves (the solid line in the diagram), while collectivists separate private and public selves while choosing a public self that is usually in harmony with the ingroup self (the broken line, above). Deviations from such general orientations readily stand out. Consider the case of the prophet.

TABLE 7
Models of the Self

PROPHETS

We learn of the prophetic role in the Bible as a collectivist cultural role. From the point of view of defined selves, what is distinctive about prophets is their willingness to have their private selves and their public selves coincide (this is also childish and childlike in collectivism, as in "The Emperor's New Clothes"). While people in these societies are expected to suppress their private selves in favor of ingroup-shaped public selves, the prophets let private and public selves coincide. So to individualist Bible readers, prophets sound honest, frank, sincere, direct. They "tell it like it is" or like it ought to be. This feature of a prophet's behavior, therefore, is not surprising to individualistic persons since this is normal individualist behavior. But such is not the case in collectivistic cultures.

One reason why a prophet must make the private self coincide with the public self is that the burden of the message is rooted in a private experience of revelation. The same is true of experiences involving dreams, visions, and stars, for example. Thus in collectivist contexts, prophets (and magi and astrologers) seem to fall into individualistic interludes in their normally collectivistic lives—interludes characterized by altered states of consciousness (see Pilch 1993b). Prophets, then, were good candidates for self-denial. But why would others in the ancient world perceive themselves as capable of denying self?

As I have noted in a previous study (Malina 1992), collectivistic persons in antiquity believed they had little if any control over their lives. They were controlled by various superordinate personages, including: God, the gods, various sky servants of God or the gods, demons, the emperor and his representatives, local kings and other elites, the wellborn, tax collectors, toll collectors, the local military, older relatives, parents, and so on. While people believed they were controlled, they often sought patrons to control those who controlled them to avoid some stressful situation. Furthermore, they may or may not have been responsible for the choices they made in such controlled contexts. Some believed they were responsible; others believed they were not.

Given this social arrangement, what type of person felt capable of changing his or her way of living? To whom would appeals for self-denial or another other form of socially based conversion be directed?

DENYING SELF: SYNOPTIC TRACES

Simply put, denial is saying "no" to something. How does one say no to the self? If the self is collectivistic, self-denial is saying no to the collectivistic self. In this section, I shall flesh out the model of collectivistic self-denial while making reference to Synoptic resonances of Jesus' injunction in these documents.

In terms of the previously sketched traits of collectivistic society, self-denial entails at least the following negations. First there is the negation of the core concern of the collectivistic self: family integrity and all that the primary ingroup provides. Given the core value of family integrity in collectivistic structures, it is no surprise that self-denial and family denial are almost parallel. In the ancient (and not so ancient) Mediterranean, females were enculturated to look forward to such dissolution of family integrity as they were handed over to another family in marriage (see Jacobs-Malina 1993). Cousin marriages turned this family denial into greater family integrity, yet such does not seem to have been the case in Hellenism (see Malina 1993). For males, on the other hand, disattachment from the family of orientation would be quite abnormal. For in a collectivistic culture, so long as a person remains in society bereft of some primary ingroup, the person remains on the brink of actual death. In this context, Judas's death follows culturally from his break with the Jesus faction because he betrayed the founder (Matt 27:3-5). In other words, survival in society after the negation of family integrity would require that a person move into some other actual or fictive kin-group. Women effected such a move without choice by marriage arrangements. On the other hand, widows were "free" (see Rom 7:2-3). Males, on the other hand, could be enticed away from their families, honorably or otherwise (for example, the prodigal younger son of Luke 15:12).

In the context of his political task, Jesus tells his self-denying core group to expect "a hundredfold now in this time, houses and brothers and sisters and mothers and children and lands" (Mark 10:29-30; see Mark 3:33-34 for Jesus' family). But in the refashioned Synoptic storyline, the outcome of such self-denial, then, would be a new ingroup and affiliation to a fictive kin-group. In the period of Jesus' activity, with focus on the revitalization of Israel, the political ingroup would consist essentially of the core group around Jesus plus faction supporters around the country, notably in Galilee (as in the "mission field" of Mark 6:6-12 and parallels). The general thrust of interpersonal relations in the post-Resurrection fictive kin-group would require that a new range of behaviors supplant the traditional collectivistic virtues. For example, while concern for ingroup honor is a traditional collectivistic virtue, the new behavior qualifying as honorable in and for the ingroup is service (for example, Mark 9:35; 10:35), attachment to other ingroup members (= love; as in Mark 12:31-33), taking the last place (Mark 10:31), and the like (see Jacobs-Malina 1993). What is now required is the adoption of new goals that might direct the pursuit of achievements which improve the position of the fictive kin-group. In this initial phase, since the Jesus group was a faction, the new goals would be those of Jesus. It might be good to recall here that a faction is a type of coalition, a group formed for a given time and for specific ends. What distinguishes a faction from other coalitions (action sets, gangs) is that a faction is personally recruited by a single person for the recruiter's own purposes. Those recruited join the faction in response to the invitation of the faction founder and to facilitate and implement the goals of the faction founder (see Malina 1988).

In a collectivistic culture, the defining attributes of a faction's core group (here: Jesus' recruits) are loyalty to the central personage(s) (called faith) and group solidarity (called love), enabling the new primary ingroup to develop survival ability until the central person's goals are realized. Jesus' goals are duly described, for example, in the "mission discourse" of Matt 10:5-42 and parallels (also "for the sake of [God's] gospel" in Mark 8:35; 10:29). Commitment to the new central personage is frequently emphasized ("for my sake" Matt 10:18, 39; 16:25; Mark 8:35; 10:29; 13:9; Luke 9:24). With this commitment at the forefront, people can see themselves sharing a common fate, now rooted in circumstances of group affiliation as Israelite "brothers" (later in baptism, as in Matt 28:19) and place of origin (for example, the first recruited are village mates from Capernaum, then presumably all Galileans), hence by ascription. Initial supporters were sought only in the house of Israel (as in Matt 10:5) and the "towns of Israel" (Matt 10:23; see also Luke 13:22). The new ingroup receives Jesus' total allegiance as his own family once did (Mark 3:31-35; Matt 12:46-50; Luke 8:19-21). Now faction members owe similar allegiance to Jesus, at least, for one cannot serve God's goals and anything or anyone else (Matt 6:24; Luke 16:11). A person's behavior toward the new ingroup is to be consistent with what the ingroup expects (see especially Matt 18:15-18, 19-20). In the New Testament period a new sort of norming gets under way as the Jesus faction adjourned only to be re-formed into a set of Jesus Messiah or Resurrected Jesus fictive kinship groups.

Behavior toward outgroups is characterized by the tendency toward maintaining distance (see the list of negative labels in Matthew compiled by Malina and Neyrey 1988: 52-154). This list, as well as various incidents in the story evidence defiance of authority (of the scribes of the Pharisees, of the Temple personnel, and later of hostile Romans), competition (with Pharisees and Judaizers), resentment of control (by the scribes of the Pharisees), formality toward outsiders, rejection of other norms, arrogant dogmatism (compare Jesus' responses to his challengers in the Synoptic tradition; Paul's responses to his opponents), and rejection of attempts by outgroups to influence the new fictive kin-group (beware of the leaven of the Pharisees).

Collectivist virtues put the emphasis on the views, needs, and goals of the new ingroup. In a faction, the emphasis falls on the views, needs, and goals of the faction founder. These include generalized reciprocity with the faction founder (Jesus heals Peter's mother-in-law without request after Jesus "calls" Peter, Mark 1:30-31), obligation and duty to the faction founder ("for my sake," listed above), security and harmony of the group (for example, "stay salty and be at peace with one another" Mark 9:50 [trans. mine]), harmony with the faction founder (those who disagree are "Satan," as Peter in Mark 8:33; Matt 16:23), obedience to the faction founder's goals ("for the [God's] gospel"), always doing what is proper (what comes "out of a person" Mark 7:20-23 and parallels), ingroup centeredness, high affiliation (followers are "brothers"), nurturance by the founder ("he saved others" Matt 15:31, prays for Peter [Luke 22:31-32]), dependency on the founder ("we are perishing" Matt 8:25; Luke 8:24), high in both superordination and subordination as the core group members find their niches (arguments about who is greatest = more honorable in Mark 9:33-35; Matt 18:1-5; Luke 9:46-48; greatest = oldest, hence precedence at Last Supper in Luke 22:24-27).

In other words, the virtues extolled by collectivist cultures will be attitudes that look to the benefit of the faction founder and his goals: the gospel of the kingdom of God. These attitudes include a sense of honor vested in core membership (to judge the tribes of Israel: Matt 19:28), respect for the faction founder ("for my sake"), other-centered behavior in support of ingroup members (service as criterion), satisfaction with one's status in the group, respect for older group members (as children in a kin-group), acceptance of one's position in the group (greatness from service), and preserving the group's public image (honor-shame ripostes). Anything that cements and supports interpersonal relationships within the ingroup is valued (service, support, ceding place). The goal of life is the founder's goal for ingroup members. Other characteristic features of collectivist cultures will be adapted to fit the life and goals of the faction. Since sexual relations are exclusively for the fulfillment of social duty, if the faction consists of adults, there will be no need for sexual relations given the temporary nature of a faction. However, once the faction takes on the more permanent form of fictive kin-group or corporate political group—such as the Pharisees had—then this changes.

The mission discourse and its implementation illustrate how social norms and obligations are defined by the founder (Mark 6:7-13; Matt 10:5-42; Luke 9:1-5) rather than determined by personal satisfaction. Followers harbor beliefs shared with the rest of the ingroup members because of their allegiance to the founder, rather than beliefs that distinguish self from ingroup. And group members value readiness to cooperate with other ingroup members in fulfilling the founder's goals; personal goals, attitudes, beliefs, and values reflect those of the founder.

Personal satisfaction does not characterize behavior in collectivist factions. The process of resocialization within the new ingroup focused in on developing habits of duty and obligation to the faction founder, sacrifice for the founder's goals, group-oriented tasks, cooperation, favoritism toward the ingroup, acceptance of ingroup authorities, nurturing, sociability, and interdependence. The outcome of such resocialization is to produce persons with emotional attachment to the faction founder, with broad concerns for the fictive kin-group and greater tendency toward ingroup cooperation and group protectiveness. Members of factions in collectivist cultures, therefore, will do what they must as dictated by the ingroup's founder rather than do what brings personal satisfaction. In conflict situations, Jesus is portrayed as expecting his collectivist followers to side with him (vertical relationships—as faction founder) over horizontal ones (others in the group who oppose, outside social equals, for example, Pharisees).

Affiliation with the Jesus faction will have to be a dyadic decision rather than a personal decision. It is interesting to note that the first followers of Jesus are actual brothers, while the third call is directed to a townmate (Matt/Levi). Whether the others in the traditional core group were related or not is not specified (although John points in some interesting directions: brothers, townmates, a twin). Since the collectivist self is a group self that internalizes group being to such an extent that members of ingroups respond automatically as ingroup norms specify— without doing any sort of utilitarian calculation— "conversion" will be possible only in terms of mini-groups and in public. John's baptisms involved such groups and Jesus belonged to one of them.

Thus Jesus calls his first followers in pairs and/or in public. Such conversion requires dislodging the perception that previous ingroup norms, the norms characteristic of Israel, are generally valid for those born in the house of Israel. This can only be done by refashioning present ingroups into outgroups (thus "hating one's family" as noted above; opposition to Pharisees, opposition to the Temple and its personnel; "he that is not against us is for us" [Mark 9:40 RSV]).

Along with rearranging group allegiances, new motivation for resocialization into the faction has to be provided. The result will have to be distrust and unwillingness to cooperate with the previous ingroups likewise bent on "pleasing God" (Pharisees, temple authorities). How would this be possible? It would seem that a number of Jesus' followers were motivated by the fact that Jesus had access to God's patronage. This patronage was extended to control those who previously controlled people's existence; note the control exerted now by the core group: "authority over unclean spirits" (Mark 6:7), or more fully: "authority over unclean spirits, to cast them out, and to heal every disease and every infirmity . . . to heal the sick, raise the dead, cleanse lepers, cast out demons" (Matt 10:1, 8 RSV). Both those sharing in such authority as well as the recipients of it would be prime candidates for self-denial. In the gospel story, Jesus' core group members believed they were responsible for their actions and that their self-denial should be rewarded (Mark 10:28-31; Matt 19:27-28). This is quite different from Paul's perspective, according to which people were really not responsible (as in Rom 5:12-17; 7:1-25). They are "called by God" (1 Cor 7:17 and elsewhere), so both their self-denying behavior and its rewards are a patronage favor of God brokered by Jesus (see Malina 1992).

Since Jesus' problem is revitalizing "the lost sheep of the house of Israel" (Matt 10:5), his faction produces a new ingroup that will be the true Israel. If the obstacle to this revitalization is kinship attachment, then the new Israel will be a new (fictive) kin-group (as in later Messiah Jesus groups). If Israel's problem is obeying and pleasing the God of Israel, the new ingroup will have these tasks as its goal. If Israel requires revitalization, it will be because it deviated in its social structures and cultural values from what it was meant to be. Such deviance was apparent in styles of adherence to temple and sacrifice rather than to God and obedience to God.

Since neither generation nor geography serves to define the self any longer, the self must be a new collectivistic person in repentant Israel. To outgroups the self is always an aspect or a representative of the ingroup that consists of related, gendered persons who come from and live in a certain place. To ingroup members, the self is still a bundle of roles, yet generation and geography are not key elements. Even John the Baptist knew God could make children of Abraham from stones (Matt 3:9; Luke 3:8). Yet one does not readily distinguish self from social role; the first followers were still fishermen, albeit "fishers of men" (Mark 1:16 and parallels). The performance of duties associated with roles is still the path to social respect. On the other hand, social perception is prismed through the other, that is, to which group he or she belongs. And the range of outgroup persons were still characterized by place of origin (for

example, Judeans, Samaritans, Jerusalemites, Galileans), group of affiliation (Pharisees, Sadduccees), and social role (priest, scribe).

Collectivist persons are concerned about the results of their actions
on others in the ingroup. The problem, of course, is the degree of self-
identity with the faction, collocated with the abiding identity with the
kin-group. Female relatives of Jesus' disciples are variously mentioned as
present with the Lord and his entourage, including at the crucifixion (see
Mark 15:40-41). Ingroup members were to share material and nonmaterial resources with group members. They were to be concerned about
how their behavior appeared to others since they believed the outcomes
of their behavior should correspond with ingroup values. The problem
that remained was which ingroup took precedence: faction or kin-
group? All ingroup members felt involved in the contributions of their
fellows and shared in their lives.

As in society at large, then, individuals would develop strong emotional attachment to the new ingroup, perceiving all group members as
relatively homogeneous, with their behavior regulated by the founder's
goals, based on acceptance of the founder's norms with a view to
ingroup harmony and achievement at the expense of outgroups. Faction
members are to treat each other like family members (Matt 18:1-4).
Since collectivism is associated with homogeneity of affect: if members
were sad in the Jesus ingroup, one was sad; if all were joyful, one was joyful. The faction founder would expect unquestioned acceptance of
ingroup goals and norms flowing from the goals and resulting in eventual homogeneity of norms, attitudes, and values. Interpersonal relations within the ingroup were seen as an end in themselves.

The perception of limited good—if something good happens to an
outgroup member it is bad for the ingroup because "good" is finite and
thus resources are always in a zero-sum distribution pattern—is found
in the Jesus group. Notice the concern about who is greatest (Mark 9:34
and parallels) and about being prominently first after Jesus (James and
John wish this in Mark 10:35-37; while it is their mother in Matt 20:20-
21). As a corollary, anyone for the outgroup is against us (see Mark 9:40;
similarly: "He who is not with me is against me, and he who does not
gather with me scatters" [Luke 11:23 RSV]).

Finally, the ingroup is responsible for the actions of its members.
This has implications for intergroup relations. Specifically, in collectivism one expects solidarity in action toward other groups. Joint action
is the norm (Jesus is often attacked through disciples, Mark 2:16 and

parallels; or disciples are attacked through Jesus, Mark 2:18, 24 and parallels). Good outcomes for the other groups are undesirable, even when they are in no way related to one's own outcomes (on the almsgiving, prayer, and fasting of Pharisees in Matt 6:1-18; or on Pharisee behavior in Matt 23:2-36). Each individual is responsible for the actions of all other ingroup members and the ingroup is responsible for the actions of each individual member (hence the need to address Judas's shameful behavior, notably in Matt 27:3-10). For instance, even regarding the broad ingroup of regional residents, Galileans relate to Judeans in response to Judean policies in Galilee as if each Judean were the maker of those policies; they interpret the actions of individual Judeans which fit their general ideological framework as the actions of all Judeans (thus the special notice of "Jerusalemite" scribes [Mark 3:22; 7:1 and parallels]; the underscored hostility of Judeans throughout Matthew, with the climax coming when Judean Jerusalemites answer: "His blood be on us and on our children!" [Matt 27:25 RSV]; the final decree of Jesus is given in Galilee, not Judea [Matt 28:16]).

While collectivists sought to maintain harmony with humans and gods, to live in harmony with the environment, Jesus' ingroup followers, with their commission to exorcise and heal, were expected to control the environment in the area of illness (and perhaps others as well). To heal another is to control those forces that made one ill (see Pilch 1993b; 2000). The purity orientation derived from Israel did not prevent new Israel from attempting to include those who were different, and to be noncompetitive within their group.

Along with other collectivist cultures, one would expect the Jesus faction to evidence high rates of social support when unpleasant life events occur. The gospel story simply reports their coming together after Jesus' death and the adjournment of the faction. The Book of Acts, in turn, describes how this faction reforms into a primary group expecting Jesus as Israel's Messiah. As primary group it was to become a normative reference group that provided strong social ties, emotional warmth, and prompt punishment for deviance as all waited. Of course it tended to be culturally homogeneous and included active gossip, frequent rites, memorable myths, a plausible ideology, and badges of membership.

Conclusion

Mainstream culture in the United States is one of self-denial by first-century standards. By those standards, the collectivistic self is dead. We, male and female, are taught to kill our collectivist inclinations through our enculturation and socialization. Note how our killing of the collectivistic self enables the individualist self to emerge in all its exaggerated glory. Instead of an over-bloated and overexaggerated collectivist self, we find ourselves sporting an over-bloated and overexaggerated individualism.

The confusions generated by perceptions typical of individualistic and collectivistic cultures are well illustrated, for example, in the eminently collectivistic encyclical of Pope John Paul II, *Splendor of the Truth*. This document places emphasis on individualism as something negative. It even advocates the elimination, debasing, and rejection of individualism. The real question is: Individualism of what sort? If the document refers to idiocentrism or self-centeredness regardless of cultural type, it would make perfect sense and would win the consent of most individualistic Americans. But if the document means the individualistic way of life of the United States, that would be difficult to take seriously, to say the least. Collectivistic cultures may have their merits, but these do not include political freedom and economic development.

In an individualistic cultural context, it would be equally difficult to implement what Jesus expected of his followers. While many find it imperative to remind Americans of the great value of family solidarity, family attachment, and family commitment, it is the denial of such a family focus that is the burden of the self-denial required by Jesus "for the kingdom." As the Synoptic tradition itself reveals, self-denial is family denial. In the post-resurrection Messianic Jesus groups, it was adherence to a fictive kin-group centered on God and adhering to the reappropriated teachings of Jesus that was to characterize true Israel.

Ancient steps leading from the western hill to the Kidron Valley to connect with the road to Gethsemane; Jerusalem, the West Bank

৩ 6 ৩

THE SOCIAL GOSPEL
OF JESUS
AND ITS OUTCOMES

Mediterranean society of the Roman *oikoumene* was a ruralized society. It seems that all ruralized societies evidence the features that give rise to patronage and ruralized societies necessarily require patron-client relations for any sort of well-being on the part of the majority population. Such societies run into crises when traditionally accessible patronage is no longer available to prospective clients. This seems to have been the situation faced by one of Israel's prophets, John the Baptist, and his successor, Jesus of Nazareth. Comparative archaeological evidence suggests that the unrest characteristic of Israel during the first part of the first century was due to unwillingness on the part of Israelite aristocratic elites to function as patrons for their fellow Israelites (their "neighbors") in favor of expanding their own elite standing. Furthermore, the construction of new cities, the remodeling of older ones, the building of new palaces and villas—all point to increased extortion on the part of elites to the detriment of their fellows (see Oakman 1985).

Significantly, Jesus' proclamation of the kingdom of God, a theocracy involving political religion as well as political economy, involved government by God. But in the Jesus tradition, the God of Israel was not monarch but patron. To what sort of question/problem/situation is Jesus' attitude toward God as Father a response/solution? The answer: To a situation requiring patronage. God is and will be Father.

As has been demonstrated by James Barr (1988), the Aramaic *'Abba* did not mean "Daddy," as it does in modern Hebrew. Both in New

Testament translation (*'Abba* = *ho Pater*; Mark 14:36; Rom 8:15; Gal 4:6) as well as from grammatical construction, *'Abba* means father, a term of respect and honor. In a patriarchy, it implies distance as well. God is not a daddy but a patron. In the political religion preached by Jesus, the God of Israel is Israel's patron.

By proclaiming the kingdom of God and God as patron, Jesus was presenting solutions to existing social problems. The kingdom of God would prevail over the widespread ills generated by a malfunctioning or nonfunctioning political system. Jesus' message urged Israelites to endure in the present and look forward to the forthcoming, new political theocracy where God would be Israel's patron.

In this chapter, I will address the following question: Since there were subsequent Jesus groups that handed on traditions about Jesus, what do these traditions intimate both about those groups and about Jesus as group founder? The traditions indicate that Jesus formed a faction with a symbolic twelve helpers to proclaim the kingdom of God and to heal in the name of the God of Israel addressed as Father. What does this imply about Jesus in his social setting? And what of later Jesus group members? It would be ethnocentric and anachronistic to broach such implications from a modern, Romantic, individualistic, psychological point of view. People before the seventeenth century were anti-introspective and not psychologically minded. Like 80 percent of the world's population today, ancient Mediterraneans were collectivistic personalities (Hofstede 1980; 1994; Malina 1994b; 1996b). Romantic, individualistic psychology will not be useful to characterize Jesus, except as a fertile field for psychological projection. I will answer the question from the viewpoint of social psychology (see Miller 1997; and Pilch 1997).

ACCOUNTING FOR THE JESUS GROUP

It is a truism in small group research that small groups emerge because some person becomes aware of a need for change and that person shares this awareness with others who mutually nurture a hope of success in implementing the change in a societal context in which group formation is expected (Zander 1985 passim; Ross and Staines 1972). Since Jesus did indeed proclaim a kingdom and looked upon God as Father, proclaiming a political, political religious, and political economic theocracy to Israel, he was aware of a solution to Israel's political problems and was in the process of sharing that solution with others. Those who heard him would compare his solution with other available solutions and, if they found it feasible, would adopt it and tell others about it. It is at this point that people would be amenable to forming a small group around Jesus. If people rejected the solution, then Jesus' proclamation would be without effect. In brief, the features of a small group formation may be summed up as: AWARE—SHARE—COMPARE—DECLARE (see Malina 1995b).

It is at this point that proper historians break out in a mental rash that reveals their allergies to social-scientific perspectives, as noted in the introduction. Historians would like inductive evidence demonstrating the existence of these stages. To postulate them would be faulty method. Yet such proper historians never reveal the implicit models that they postulate and employ for collecting what they believe to be evidence. They have never yet demonstrated that all ancient peoples had lungs, a heart, veins, and arteries. They presume the ancients were biological beings as we are and that their natural biological functioning was like our own. Then why the hesitancy with regard to basic social patterns when such patterns have in fact been verified cross-culturally? The problem is, have they been verified cross-temporally? Social historians prefer the rational harmony of their social history—they tell us the way things must have been because it makes sense. I would prefer the irrational stability of social-scientific interpretation—the way things must have been derives from a fit with the cultural script of the region in question.

Just as knowledge of contemporary human biology offers models for understanding the past by providing questions about life in the past, the same is true for contemporary, cross-culturally verified social patterns. While there may not be many such patterns on the planet, there are two relevant ones for this inquiry: first, the previously noted pattern of small group formation as the outcome of some person's problem solving; second, a pattern of small group development.

Consider the pattern of a person's awareness of a solution to some problem that lies at the bottom of any group formation. For a small group to emerge, there must be 1) conditions favorable for change, 2) along with a vision of a new situation, 3) coupled with hope relative to implementing that situation successfully, and 4) all this in a social system that has problem solving groups. These are the facilitating circumstances for the creation of any group. Since a group emerged around Jesus, obviously all four of these dimensions were present. Consider each in turn.

1. Presence of Change Conditions

Change conditions refer to people's desire for social satisfaction. General awareness of unsatisfactory social conditions point to change conditions. The formation of any group is always rooted in some individuals' desire for change perceived as feasible due to the presence of conditions favorable for change. For John the Baptist and Jesus, the condition was an ineffective patronage system, with Israel's elites ignoring prospective clients. Israel's aristocrats did not fulfill their social obligations. Institutional arrangements had to be changed.

A potential organizer such as Jesus in Galilee had to have sufficient social standing and ability to define the prevailing undesirable state of affairs. Israel's political system was rooted in the Torah. Torah study was socialization into the main values and structures of the society. By the second century B.C.E. the Torah came to be regarded not as the highest expression of the religious consciousness of a particular age, but as the full and final utterance of the mind of God—adequate, infallible, and valid for all eternity. While the Law thus came to be regarded as all-sufficient for time and eternity, alike as an intellectual creed, a liturgical system, and a practical guide in ethics and religion, there was practically no room left for new light or interpretation or for any further disclosure of God's will—in short there was no room for the true prophet, but only for the moralist, the casuist, and the preacher. (Charles 1913: 2–3)

Adequate social standing to challenge prevailing Torah applications was available to prophets, priests, and kings, the usual recipients of divine revelation (Luke 10:24; Matt 13:17 changes it). It seems kings at the time made no claim to such revelation while the Sadducean priesthood might claim it when necessary (as Luke 1:67 states of Zechariah, and John 11:49-53 intimates of Caiaphas; Israelite prophets: Luke 2:26: Simeon, v. 36: Anna). Those with prophetic call were compelled to resort to pseudonymity, issuing the divine commands with which they were entrusted under the name of some ancient worthy in Israel. But with the advent of John the Baptist, non-pseudonymous Israelite prophecy was revitalized.

Prophets were frequent in later Jesus Messiah groups. There is generic reference to prophets in Paul (Gal 1:15-16; 1 Cor 12:10; Rom 12:6), Matthew (7:15; 24:11) and Luke-Acts (Acts 2:15-21, quoting Joel 2:28-32), for example. Individuals described as prophets or as playing a prophetic role are characterized as having an altered state of consciousness experience (see Pilch 1993b). Jesus and his baptism experience

(Mark 1:9-11; Luke 3:21-22), John at the baptism of Jesus (Matt 3:13-37 and John 1:32-34), Peter with his multiple visions in Acts (10:9-17, 19-20—a vision in a trance, explained again in 11:4-18; 12:6-11); Paul and his call (Gal 1:15-16; Acts 9:1-19; 22:3-21; 26:9-20; also Acts 16:9-10; 18:9-10), Ananias and his vision (Acts 9:10-16), Agabus and his messages (Acts 11:28-29; 21:10-11), John the Seer and his visions (Rev 1:3, 10; like Stephen in Acts 7:55-56, cf. Acts 1:10-11 of the Twelve), are all instances of persons perceived as prophets. In first-century Israel and in the Jesus tradition there were prophets who offered solutions to social problems. The Jesus tradition begins with one such prophet named John the Baptist.

John's activity was rooted in the realization that Israel's social situation was not what it might be and that something ought to be done about it. In the Synoptic story, it was John the Baptist who presumably suggested this realization to Jesus (clearly articulated by Matt 3:1—4:17, presumably thanks to Mark 1:1-14; Luke 3:1—5:11 describes it differently). All evidence points to Jesus in the entourage of John the Baptist. Jesus was a member of John's group (Hollenbach 1982b). A group is a collection of persons who gather for some specific reason. People gathered around John, we are told, for the sake of a symbolic dipping underscoring their willingness to get their affairs in order within the political/domestic framework of Israel's daily life. The Q reports about John's advice indicate concern for political religion (Q 3:7-9), while Luke underlines political economy and political religion (Luke 3:10; see Esler 1987). All traditions state that Jesus took part in John's symbolic dipping and imply that he underwent an altered state of consciousness experience in which God called Jesus "son." Jesus had an experience of God as Father (thus Mark 1:9-11 and Luke 3:21-22). By using the usual fictive kinship terminology of the day, God addressed Jesus as his client. Their political religious relationship was "kin-ified." John the Baptist, then, was a broker who put individuals, in this case Jesus, in contact with the God of Israel. Only Matthew reports that John's behavior related to a forthcoming theocracy: "the kingdom of heaven is at hand" (John 3:2 RSV).

Jesus' positive response to John's summons to baptism implies that Jesus compared the merits of John's proclamation and was convinced by it. This compare stage points to some societal trigger state. The trigger state arouses individuals to take action, to join a group, and to work to maintain it. A trigger state converts a social situation into motivational material. For example, an unjust act may be converted into striving for a just social order or some grievance against an authority into desire to eliminate the grievance (consider the Intifada on the West Bank and in Gaza or the activity of the Hizbollah freedom fighters in Lebanon). In the case of Jesus, we are not informed about the trigger that brought him to John. On the other hand, we are well informed about the trigger that led him on his own prophetic career: the arrest of John by Herod (Mark 1:14-15 and parallels). The situation that had to be changed, as John intimated, was some feature of social behavior prevailing in Israel. The Synoptic tradition indicates that Jesus shared this awareness of John the Baptist. Both proclaimed the need for getting one's life in order and the onset of God's running Israel ("Repent for the kingdom of God is at hand" Matt 4:17; Mark 1:15; implied by Luke 4:43).

Thus the tradition indicates that after John's arrest, Jesus took up John's program, but he moved a step further. No longer confined to the riverbank, Jesus moved into populated areas, making the same proclamation but with something added. His new take on this theocracy was that God was Father, patron.

If people gathered around John and later around Jesus, it was because they found what they heard to be useful and meaningful. John and later Jesus proclaimed what they did because they too found their prophetic insights useful and meaningful. Jesus further departed from John's style and strategy by seeking assistance. The existence of a group recruited by Jesus indicates that Jesus believed a specific situation should be changed and that one person acting alone could not create that change. Individuals joined the core group of the Jesus movement by invitation (Mark 1:16-20; Matt 4:13-17; Luke 5:1-11). The invitation was the trigger for core group members. It was the social situation serving as motivation. Invitation was required to underscore the honor of being asked to join (Malina 1993: 29–54). Since they did in fact join, they too believed a specific situation should be changed and that Jesus acting alone could not create that change. From what ensued, we find that the specific situation was informing Israelites of God's plan to take over the country and to prepare Israelites for participation in the new situation.

2. Vision of the New Situation

Group organizers had to offer a vision of a subsequent satisfactory state of affairs. A potential group organizer does not simply perceive something to be wrong which requires change. Rather, a group developer foresees how things could be improved and successfully transmits this vision to others. A single person often envisions these better possibilities and others are then invited to improve on the plan and to join its activities.

Jesus' plan, rooted in John's activity, was clearly in mind as he recruited a number of core associates, but we are given details of the plan only when he sets his coalition into performing his own chosen task of proclaiming and healing (Mark 6:7-13; Matt 10:1-11; Luke 9:1-5). In a sense, all of Jesus' teaching about the kingdom of God was directed to describing scenarios of the subsequent state of affairs, when God takes over control of the country (frequently in Synoptics).

3. Hope for Success

Organizers and group members believed their joint actions would succeed if they tried to achieve the goal of a better state of affairs. Members joined because they believed that the satisfactory state of affairs would come about (cf. discussions on rewards Mark 10:28-31; Matt 19:27-30; Luke 18:28-30—appropriated; on sitting next to Jesus: Matt 20:20-23—mother; Mark 10:35-40; not in Luke; general storming: Mark 10:41-44; Matt 20:24-27; Luke 22:24-27). For peasants in bad situations, such belief is not hard to come by. After all, the peasant approach to life is nothing ventured, nothing gained. An organizer's efforts will fail unless the organizer trusts that the group's activities will create the desired end and unless the organizer gets adherents to believe the same. And Jesus' healing and exorcizing worked to this end. As group leader, he was responsible for building confidence in the organization. Often he did this by making it possible for members to build their own trust in him, since he was the collective self representing the group's fate (see Hollenbach 1982a).

Jesus got his core group to successfully proclaim and heal along with him. Their successes pointed to the group's achievement potential (Mark 6:12-13; Luke 9:6; 10:17-20). Participants then developed confidence in their group by their active participation and success in realizing the group's objectives. The growth of crowds following Jesus, the spread of his reputation, all underscore group success (frequently noted in the Synoptics).

4. Societal Context

If groups are to exist in a society, then the society in question must offer its members the option of forming groups. Societal conditions favoring group formation are called promoters. Persons are more likely to form a group if sources of influence foster such a move or at least offer little resistance to it. Given the presence of the preceding three conditions, interest in creating and joining a group tended to be greatest if the environs were stimulating; that is, if people lived in a complex society where groups were common and valued. For Galilee and Judea of Jesus' day, the presence of Pharisee, Sadducee, Herodian, Essene, and other groups point to such an environment. The circumstances affecting the formation of the Jesus movement group would be similar to those affecting political action groups (see Horsley and Hanson 1985).

The fact that there was a Jesus group points to a society in which people were willing: 1) to join groups, 2) to tolerate ambiguity during the early days of a group's life, 3) to favor values in the society that supported Jesus' program, 4) to forgo interest in keeping things just as they are, and 5) to develop the knowledge and skill needed for being a group member.

On the other hand, many did not respond to Jesus and his group, even though they saw the need for change. Reasons for this include their inability to share the envisioned solution and see any hope for success or their social ties to persons representing the status quo. It was perhaps such inabilities that led Jesus to avoid cities and stay in the countryside. Judean and Galilean city elites and their retainers would not be interested. City elites, of course, could not believe in any better state of affairs, so they would not be willing to accept the Jesus movement ideology. In fact, their values opposed those bound up with a forthcoming theocracy. Since city elites rejected such a vision, their retainers supported them in collectivistic fashion.

For the Jesus group, the purpose behind their faction was to have Israelites get their lives in order as preparation for God's forthcoming takeover of the country. The goal was political. Jesus organized his group because he was not satisfied with the social situation. As a recognized prophet he had enough social standing to define the undesirable state of affairs, to envision a successful alternative, to gives others hope for success—in a society that prepared people for group roles. The envisioned better state of affairs is the group's purpose or objective.

Stages of Small Group Development

The foregoing considerations serve as a sort of unzipping device to expand the high context reference to the fact that Jesus proclaimed the kingdom of God with God as Father. The onset of Jesus' activity led to his recruiting a core group of persons to assist him in his task. This core group was a faction, that is, a group of persons personally recruited by Jesus to assist in a specific task for a specific time. The summons to "come follow me" was not a call to embark on a new way of life, but a personal call for help in a task for a given time. Once the task was over, the group would be dissolved and people would go home. How did the Jesus faction develop over time? This point is important for appreciating the Jesus tradition in the New Testament since it was the original Jesus faction that initially transmitted this tradition.

Group development is about changes in the group as a whole over time as well as changes in the relationship between the group and each of its members. Cross-cultural studies of small groups has produced the following model of the stages that small groups trace over time, with verifiably predictable behavior at each stage. The stages are: forming, storming, norming, performing, and adjourning (based on the work of Tuckman [1965] and further corroborated by Moreland and Levine [1988]). Consider each of these.

1. Forming

The forming stage is the period when the group is put together. Groups are formed either to accomplish some extragroup task or for intragroup social support. The faction recruited by Jesus was a group with an extragroup task to perform. The task activity of this group is articulated in the Synoptic tradition in the mission charge: to proclaim God's taking over the country soon, to urge Israelites to get their affairs in order to this end, and to heal those in need of healing. Mark implies that group members with healing ability were chosen (Mark 3:15 and 6:7 mention only that

Jesus gave the Twelve authority over unclean spirits, yet when they return "they . . . anointed with oil many that were sick and healed them" 6:13 RSV). Matt 10:6 and Luke 9:1 (10:9 is unclear on this score), on the other hand, state that Jesus bestowed this healing ability on his recruits. During the forming stage, group members discuss the nature of their task and how it might be performed. The behavior of group members toward each other is tentative; commitment to the group is low.

2. Storming

At the storming stage, persons invited to join the group jockey for position and ease into interpersonal stances. Members of task activity groups such as the Jesus faction resist the need to work closely with one another. Conflict among members emerges, with emotions gaining free expression. Group members at this stage become more assertive and each tries to change the group's purposes to satisfy personal needs. Resentment and hostilities erupt among group members with differing needs. Each member attempts to persuade the others to adopt group goals that will fulfill his or her needs. The behavior of group members toward one another is assertive, and their commitment to the group is higher than it was before.

In the Synoptics we have many reminders of this phase: the dispute about who is greatest (Mark 9:33-37; Matt 18:1-5; Luke 9:46-48); a general argument about precedence (Mark 10:41-44; Matt 20:24-27; Luke 22:24-27); concern for sitting next to Jesus in the kingdom (Matt 20:20-23—mother; Mark 10:35-40; not in Luke); and the general concern about rewards (Mark 10:28-31; Matt 19:27-30; Luke 18:28-30—appropriated). Peter's rebuking Jesus after talk about suffering and death is an attempt to persuade Jesus to change his goals to fit what the group is concerned about (Mark 8:32-33; Matt 16:22-23; not in Luke).

3. Norming

The norming stage is marked by interpersonal conflict resolution in favor of mutually agreed upon patterns of behavior. This phase is one of exchange in task activity groups such as the Jesus faction. Everyone in the group shares ideas about how to improve the group's level of performance. Norming involves group members in the attempt to resolve earlier conflicts, often by negotiating clearer guidelines for group behavior.

The norms for Jesus' core group are listed in the mission discourse (Matt 10:5-16 and expanded with vv. 17-25; Mark 6:7-11; see 3:13-15; Luke 9:1-5).

4. Performing

In the performing stage, group participants carry out the program for which the group was assembled. Performing marks the problem-solving stage of task activity groups. Members solve their performance problems and work together productively.

From the evidence provided in the New Testament documents, it is clear that the Jesus faction moved into a performing stage (return from successful task performance: Mark 6:12-13; Luke 9:6; no report in Matthew). The sending of the seventy(-two) and their success (Luke 10:1-20) points to enlarged activity. This implies further recruitment or forming, with subsequent storming and norming to lead to greater performing.

5. Adjourning

With adjourning, group members gradually disengage from task activities in a way that reflects their efforts to cope with the approaching end of the group.

In the gospel story, the performing phase comes to a rather abrupt end, marked by the crucifixion of Jesus. Regarding Jesus' core group, the post-crucifixion stories liberally attest to preparations for adjourning, quashed by the experience of the appearance of the risen Jesus. With this experience, a feedback loop enters the process with new storming, norming, and subsequent performing, as described telescopically in the final sections of Matthew and Luke, but at length in the opening of Acts. The trigger event for this loopback was the core group's experience of Jesus after his death, an experience understood as the work of God, now perceived as "He who raised Jesus from the dead" (Acts 3:15; Rom 8:11). God thus indicated Jesus is Israel's forthcoming Messiah.

The new storming among the remaining Jesus group members led to what I shall call a Jesus Messiah group. For this group, political concerns were still at the forefront in the reports of the Gospels and Acts. But the mention of "brothers and sisters" in Jesus organizations, reflected in the Gospels as well as in Pauline communities, points to a shift from political religion to domestic religion of a fictive kinship sort. The ideology of the fictive kinship groups emerging from the political Jesus Messiah group changes in scope and purpose. I call these emerging groups Messianic Jesus groups and Resurrected Jesus groups. Briefly, Messianic Jesus groups, located in Israelite populated areas, observed Israelite exclusivity rules, awaiting the eventual coming of Jesus as Messiah while living as social support groups. Resurrected Jesus groups, found among non-Israelite populations, considered Jesus as God's new revelation, as cosmic Lord, and lived as social support groups "in Christ." The telling of the story of Jesus took features from both the experience of Messianic Jesus groups and Resurrected Jesus groups. The latter marked an institutional transformation of Jesus movement groups, from politics to (fictive) kinship.

I concur with Moreland and Levine that "most theories of group socialization implicitly assume that the group is in the performing stage of development" (1988: 164). This of course is the situation in studies of early Messianic Jesus and Resurrected Jesus groups, whether of "wandering apostles," Pauline communities, or the groups responsible for our Gospels. Our New Testament documents themselves come from storming and norming situations for the most part and are studied by scholars in performing (or adjourning) phases. Furthermore, the documents are used in churches that are into performing. It is clear that inattention to this state of affairs can lead to some theological distortion due to a sort of source critical Doppler effect.

SMALL GROUP FOCUSES

Small groups always have a purpose that consists of the perception of some needed and meaningful change. The required and desired change may be seen to inhere in persons, in groups, or in society at large. Consequently, small groups form to support and advance intrapersonal, interpersonal, intragroup, or extragroup change, or a combination of these. Extragroup objectives are directed toward changing nonmembers or even society at large. Groups with extragroup objectives are also called instrumental groups. Intragroup objectives are reflexive objectives, looking to change members of the group itself. Groups with intragroup objectives are often called expressive groups.

The Jesus Group and the Jesus Messiah Group

The group recruited by Jesus was an instrumental group, a faction with extragroup objectives. The gospel tradition tells of the Jesus group with a mission to Israelite society as a whole, to Galilee as well as to Perea and Judea. Similarly, the Jesus Messiah group that emerged with Jesus' post-crucifixion appearances was an instrumental group, a coalition with the task of letting all Israel know that Jesus was Israel's Messiah, soon to come with power. When the change envisioned by a group is societal, the change involved is a social movement. The group supporting and implementing the change is a social movement organization (see Gamson 1992).

The Jesus group was a social movement organization, specifically a political action faction. The successor group, reorganized around the ideology of Jesus as Israel's soon-returning Messiah, was equally a politically oriented social movement organization. But later Jesus groups organized in terms of fictive brothers and sisters in Christ, with an ideology claiming the resurrected Jesus to be God's new revelation for Israel, even for non-Israel. These were not social movement organizations. They were expressive groups, social support groups, forming elective associations (Kleijwegt 1994; see also Wilken 1971; Barton and Horsley 1981; Barton 1992). A consideration of social movements and social movement organizations will indicate the main difference between the Jesus movement and its successor, the Jesus Messiah movement, on the one hand, and those rather different fictive kinship groups, the Messianic Jesus groups and the Resurrected Jesus groups, on the other.

> A social movement is a set of opinions and beliefs in a population representing preferences for changing some elements of the social structure or reward distribution, or both, of a society. Persons who embrace the opinions and beliefs of a social movement and guide their lives accordingly form a social movement group or organization (McCarthy and Zald 1987: 20).

The movement that Jesus launched was a social movement; Jesus' own group was a social movement organization. Group members worked to change "elements of the social structure or reward distribution, or both, of a society." The Jesus Messiah groups described in the early chapters of Acts expected such change when Jesus returned as Messiah with power—as political personage.

But the subsequent groups founded by those change agents called "wandering apostles" were not social movement groups at all, since their purpose was not to change "elements of the social structure or reward distribution, or both, of a society." Instead, the fictive kingroups founded by these apostles looked to salvation, the cosmic rescue of collectivistic persons of the first-century Mediterranean world. Their new outlook was replicated in kinship space, the house (see White 1982). These fictive kingroups were of two types: those located among densely Israelite populations, which I call Messianic Jesus groups, and those located among sparsely Israelite populations, which I call Resurrected Jesus groups. The former Messianic Jesus groups were largely described as among the circumcised, while the latter, the Resurrected Jesus groups, were typically found among the uncircumcised (Gal 2:7-9). The former were like Israelite purity-oriented groups (for example, the Pharisees), while the latter were most like Greco-Roman clubs and *collegia*, equally concerned with the social well-being of collective selves.

To return to the Jesus social movement, it is important to note that social movements invariably stand along with countermovements, that is, "a set of opinions and beliefs in a population opposed to a social movement" (McCarthy and Zald 1987: 20; see also Messick and Mackie 1989). In the scenarios of the Jesus story, countermovement organizations were equally present: Pharisees, Sadducees, Herodians, and others.

Countermovements focus on stability and permanence. In contrast to new groups arising to solve newly perceived problems, members of countermovement organizations make a point of holding to the same purposes indefinitely. The easiest way to insist upon such permanence is to make eligibility for membership reside in birth. In that way, prospective members can be duly socialized to fit into permanency patterns. Sadducees rooted in aristocratic families, Pharisees rooted in Abrahamic pedigree, and Herodians rooted in a monarchic family, all clearly aim at well-guarded permanence. This is an officialdom based on birth, with political religion rooted initially in kinship, then in the body politic co-opted by some ruling kinship group.

Such groups normally underscore the value of stability and tend to establish methods that protect against attempts to change objectives. The Sadducees insisted on the charter of Israel's political religion, the Torah, but only as relevant and applicable in their day. The Pharisees allowed for a growing tradition that must necessarily fit the practice of the ancients. The Herodians focused on a single set of properly rooted heirs. In all cases, they have established doctrine, ceremonies that ask participants to revere an unchanging set of beliefs, a society pledging faith to its charter, and staffs that lay plans that fit respective special systems of behavior. Each group's firmness of purpose was duly guarded by officials who trained members not to doubt the aims of the organization and who punished persons who deviated from the set's objectives. Israel's politically embedded religious bodies were particularly likely to police the behavior of members in this way.

They insisted on interpretations of Torah in terms that were familiar to them. As members of the house of Israel, they pressed officials to retain the aims of the past. While under Roman control a number of monarchic or priestly agencies may have disappeared, but interested parties sought to make sure that their purposes were preserved. The initial objectives were passed on to a body whose life was continuing. The disembodied purposes were thus transplanted and kept vital because Israelite elites who benefited from the government's activities pressed their representatives to maintain support for the objectives. The agencies of political religion were not immortal, but their purposes appear to have been.

Some objectives remained unchanged and did not emerge as a source of concern because there was no way to tell whether the group was moving toward desired ends. Does Torah observance in Sadducee or Pharisee style actually please God? Does it produce righteousness among group members? Does scribal study of Torah further Pharisee or Sadducee purity? Do these groups actually help the house of Israel by their way of life? Questions like these were hard to answer and members could only guess whether their goals were being satisfied. Participants most often estimated that the group's objective was being satisfactorily fulfilled and ought not be changed because looking elsewhere for success was less attractive than anticipating failure (Zander 1971). In the story of Jesus, it was precisely these kinds of questions that were in the forefront of countermovement conflict.

Lenses for Reading the Historical Jesus in the Gospels

The problem in historical Jesus study is to disentangle the period and concerns of the original Jesus group from successor groups. In this chapter I identify three groups that succeed the original Jesus faction—the political coalition that I call the Jesus Messiah group, and its two fictive kinship successors, the Messianic Jesus groups and the Resurrected Jesus groups. The earlier discussion about group formation and small group development provides the following comparative insights for reading about the historical Jesus in the Gospels (Table 8).

So long as post-Jesus groups remained in the territory of the "circumcised" (Judea, Perea, Galilee, large Judean quarters in nearby cities such as Antioch or Alexandria), they remained in conflict with countermovement organizations of Israelite origin and adhered to their political purpose. After all, only Israel had messiahs, and Jesus was Israel's messiah soon to come with power. The mention of power points to the political institution as focal. When Jesus comes as Israel's messiah with power, a theocracy will be inaugurated and the kingdom will be experienced by all Israel, including Israelites of all nations as listed in Acts 2:4. Dedicated Jesus Messiah group members, often known as wandering apostles, brought this information to Israelite colonies spread over the Mediterranean, traveling from Judean quarter to Judean quarter in city after city—so the picture in Acts. But in Acts, the context remains political religion to the very end: Paul in Rome is still proclaiming the kingdom (Acts 28:31). Even the paradigmatic coming of the non-Israelite Cornelius to the Jesus Messiah group centered in Peter is assessed in terms of political religion (Acts 10:1-48). In the political charter of Israel, the Torah, there are rules for resident aliens (Lev 17:8, 10, 13; 18:26) that could be applied to Gentiles, as in the decrees of the Jerusalem Council (15:20-21; repeated in vv. 28-29). However, it eventually dawned upon some in the Jesus Messiah group that these ethnic outsiders were not resident aliens everywhere. While in Judea and Galilee (or even Alexandria and Antioch, perhaps) they may have been aliens, but in cities outside traditional Israelite territory, they were the residents. It was the Israelites who were the resident aliens there.

A resulting new social structure in "uncircumcised" regions emerges not as a variant on political religion, but as domestic religion. What of nonethnic Israelites? In domestic religion there is no room for the political category of resident aliens. But there is room for Israel's exclusivity rules, of no mixing with outsiders. So who are the few Gentiles in their midst? One successor to the Israelite-based Jesus Messiah group would insist on rules of no mixing with the Gentiles. In effect, non-Israelite males who wished to join the group would have to be circumcised and follow Israel's kosher rules as they were among "the circumcised." I call these Messianic Jesus groups. These were fictive kinship groups of brothers and

JESUS GROUPS	JESUS MESSIAH GROUPS	MESSIANIC JESUS GROUPS	RESURRECTED JESUS GROUPS
• A political faction recruited by Jesus	• Political coalition awaiting Israel's messiah	• Fictive kin-groups expecting Jesus as Israel's messiah	• Fictive kin-groups living "in Christ"
• Task-oriented: to inform Israel about the coming kingdom of God and to prepare Israel	• Task oriented: to let all Israel know Jesus is Israel's Messiah, soon to come in power	• Social support oriented: Torah focused, awaiting Israel's messiah and promised Israelite theocracy	• Social support oriented: living "in Christ" with newly developing norms
• Trigger: arrest of John the Baptist	• Trigger: resurrection appearances of Jesus	• Trigger: alternate state of consciousness experiences of prophets like Agabus, witness of Stephen, death of James, Judean customs in Israel	• Trigger: alternate state of consciousness experiences of prophets like Paul, coming of non-Israelites unsolicited, Judean customs in various Greco-Roman cities
• Solution: proclaim kingdom of God as Patron; heal, exorcise, prepare Israel	• Solution: proclaim Jesus as Israel's messiah soon to return and inaugurate God's kingdom	• Solution: the Way a way of living Torah in fictive kin-groups, appropriating Jesus' teaching to this end	• Solution: live peaceably with all, with fictive kin-groups for social support
• Vision: the kingdom of God is like . . .	• Vision: God will take control of Israel soon	• Vision: living according to Jesus Messiah's *halakah* until he comes in judgment	• Vision: cosmic meaning, belonging, and comfort in God revealed in the resurrection of Jesus
• Hope of success rooted in successes in proclaiming and healing	• Hope of success rooted in success in proclaiming Jesus as Israel's messiah and healing	• Hope of success rooted in alternate state of awareness experiences, mutual support, and new way of life in Israel	• Hope of success rooted in alternate states of awareness experiences, mutual support, and new way of life in Christ
• A type of Israelite political action group	• A type of Israelite political action group	• A type of Israelite fictive kin-group, an elective association (like Pharisee *haburoth*, Essene group)	• A type of Greco-Roman fictive kin-group, an elective association (*collegium*, guild)
• Purpose: have Israelites get their lives in order in preparation for theocracy; political	• Purpose: have Israelites get their lives in order in preparation for the messiah's coming	• Purpose: have Israelites who expect Jesus as Israel's Messiah live in the new righteousness	• Purpose: have Israelites and others called by God live "in Christ" with mutual support

Table 8 continued on next page

JESUS GROUPS	JESUS MESSIAH GROUPS	MESSIANIC JESUS GROUPS	RESURRECTED JESUS GROUPS
• The group develops through all five stages: forming, storming, norming, performing, and on the brink of adjourning	• A feedback loop to new storming and norming and per-forming: proclaiming Jesus to Israel as Israel's messiah	• A feedback loop to new storming and norming; uncertain performing is ingroup oriented, with empha-sis on waiting watch-fully	• A feedback loop to new storming and norming; uncertain performing is ingroup oriented, with empha-sis on proper behavior and ingroup attach-ment
• Change sought is extra-group: transitive objectives to change Israel at large	• Change sought is extra-group: transitive objectives to change Israel at large	• Change sought is intragroup: intransi-tive goals to live the new righteousness	• Change sought is intragroup: intransi-tive goals to live "in Christ" with mutual support
• Social movement organization with countermovement organizations in Israel	• Social movement organization with countermovement organizations in Israel	• Elective association consisting largely of Israelites, with fre-quent conflict with fellow Israelites	• Elective association consisting largely of Israelites and a num-ber of non-Israelites; ingroup conflicts as well as conflicts with Israelites

TABLE 8
Group Formation

sisters faithful to Israel's Torah and Israel's Messiah, Jesus. In the new domestic context, Jesus is a teacher of a new way of life that group members live with a view to acquiring the new righteousness. To follow Jesus meant to live this new way of life. Thus the political matrix drops out. Instead we have all sorts of analogies derived from the kinship institution now used to describe the experience of God among those awaiting Israel's Messiah. Patronage and grace are still there. There is still favor. But it is no longer favor in a political key, but favor in a domestic key. Patronage helps people understand the new institutional reality, since patronage "kin-ifies" relations between patron and client in a domestic institutional framework. This is domestic religion! The Gospel of Matthew gives clearest expression to the ideology of this sort of Mes-sianic Jesus group.

Another successor to the Israelite-based Jesus Messiah group took on a range of viewpoints shared by Israelites, called "Judeans" by the Romans, who lived as distinct minorities among "the uncircumcised." For Jesus Messiah group members who found themselves outside Israelite-populated areas, the experience of the resurrected Jesus led to the same change in the social structure of Jesus Messiah groups as with

Messianic Jesus groups. For a long time Israelite groups living among the uncircumcised took on the shape of fictive kinship groups of brothers and sisters in Israel. What kept them in contact with the political religion of Israel was their temple tax and, for some, the pilgrimage. For a number of these Israelites, the acceptance of Jesus as Israel's Messiah led them to replace their relationships with their brothers and sisters in Israel with a new relationship with brothers and sisters in Israel's Messiah, brothers and sisters in Christ.

These are the Resurrected Jesus groups, as I call them. In the ideology of these groups, the resurrected Jesus was a new revelation of God to Israel. Jesus was cosmic lord, cosmic broker or mediator before the God of Israel, and called by God for all. And since God's call might now be directed to all persons in the empire, God could now be conceived as the God of the *oikoumene*, a truly monotheistic God.

This is a radical departure from the movement that Jesus started. But for Jesus group members, this is what God has wrought, through his power, the Spirit. It was God who called the non-Israelites to Jesus Messiah groups. And it was God who revealed himself in the groups' experiences of the resurrected Jesus. For Messianic Jesus groups (Matthew), the risen Messiah was living verification of the way of life of these groups. To follow Jesus was to seek righteousness in terms of Jesus' Torah interpretation as all await Jesus' coming as Israel's Messiah with power. For Resurrected Jesus groups (see the later Paul, the earlier Paul: 1 Thess 2:12), the resurrected Jesus was the new "burning bush" experience. While focus on theocracy dwindled, many statements concerning the theocracy and its behavioral requirements lived on. Thus a number of Pauline statements on who is to enter the kingdom certainly trace back to a time when political religious Jesus Messiah groups strongly awaited the Messiah with power (Rom 14:17; 1 Cor 4:20; 6:9-10; 15:50; Gal 5:21; even Eph 5:5). But with Paul and his Resurrected Jesus groups, the political, theocratic impact of such statements was lost. With the development of Messianic Jesus groups in Israelite enclaves and of Resurrected Jesus groups around the Mediterranean, a development ascribed to the promptings and direction of God, Jesus' political religious movement was transformed into a domestic religious association. Such domestic religion was fictive kinship religion expressed as a "household of faith" (Gal 6:10 RSV).

Conclusion

One of the key problems in a considerate reading of the New Testament is the understanding of the world that the reader brings to the task. A considerate reading would have the reader attempt to share in the scenarios of the author. For a considerate reading of the New Testament, a reader must use scenarios in which political religion and/or domestic religion figure prominently. Any scenario that filters out or excludes ancient Mediterranean political and domestic relations and values as peripheral to New Testament understanding will have to be at least anachronistic, certainly ethnocentric. A considerate reading of the New Testament requires readers to envision Jesus' social movement as religion configured by the parameters and concerns of politics. Similarly, subsequent Jesus group associations will be envisioned as religion configured by the parameters and concerns of kinship. For it was in terms of face-to-face and face-to-mace interactions of a political and kinship sort that the Jesus movement and subsequent Jesus Messiah groups articulated their faith in the one God of all.

Parallel to the embedded and disembedded social institutions of economics and religion, persons bonded with each other in terms of face-to-face interactions, face-to-mace interactions, and face-to-space interactions. Face-to-face interactions were rooted in kinship; it was kinship modes of face-to-face interaction that provided the social matrix for dealing with the larger world. Face-to-mace interactions are agency-extended in nature. They emerged with the disembedding of politics from kinship. As politics became a freestanding institution, persons interacted with controllers of collective effective action and their power sanctions in terms of intermediaries or agents of the central power holder(s).

Finally, some human societies witness disembodied-extended interactions. With the emergence of the nation-state, with the nation becoming a fully imaginary entity, persons interact with representations (and not representatives) of controllers of collective effective action and with representations of their agents as well—in terms of printed messages, newspapers, television, and similar communications. Even interaction with the agents of centralized political entities now entails dealing with an impersonal bureaucracy, often through media that keep the interacting parties at a distance (phone, letters, the Internet, etc.).

In summary, the human community on this planet based its normal interactions with those that controlled its existence—first personally, then through representatives, and finally through representations. Representatives, physically present, were viewed as agents and concrete substitutes for the person with whom one sought to interact. Finally, representations themselves are considered concrete substitutes for the presence of the person in question.

The kingdom of God was to take the form of personal and representative theocracy. In these dimensions it would have had the same structure as the political religion of Israel during the time of Jesus. The open question was: Who would be the agent, the concrete substitute for the God of Israel? Jesus group members had little doubt that that agent would be Jesus, the Messiah of Israel. But God had more in mind than Israel alone.

ABBREVIATIONS

AmAnth	*American Anthropologist*
AJS	*American Journal of Sociology*
AmSocRev	*American Sociological Review*
ANRW	*Aufstieg und Niedergang der römischen Welt*
AnthQ	*Anthropological Quarterly*
ARA	*Annual Reviews in Anthropology*
ARP	*Annual Review of Psychology*
BibInt	*Biblical Interpretation*
BibIntSer	Biblical Interpretation Series
BTB	*Biblical Theology Bulletin*
CBQ	*Catholic Biblical Quarterly*
CCL	*Corpus Christianorum Latinorum*
CSSH	*Comparative Studies in Society and History*
CQ	*Classical Quarterly*
CurAnth	*Current Anthropology*
CurTM	*Currents in Theology and Mission*
ExpT	*Expository Times*
FSE	*Forum for Social Economics*
GBS	Guides to Biblical Scholarship
Gr.	Greek
Heb.	Hebrew
HTR	*Harvard Theological Review*
IJP	*International Journal of Psychoanalysis*
JAC	*Jahrbuch für Antike und Christentum*
JAAR	*Journal of the American Academy of Religion*
JAnthR	*Journal of Anthropological Research*
JCCP	*Journal of Cross-Cultural Psychology*
JECS	*Journal of Early Christian Studies*
JEL	*Journal of Economic Literature*

JPSP	*Journal of Personality and Social Psychology*
JRH	*Journal of Religious History*
JRS	*Journal of Roman Studies*
JSNT	*Journal for the Study of the New Testament*
JSNTSup	Journal for the Study of the New Testament Supplement Series
JSOTSup	Journal for the Study of the Old Testament Supplement Series
JTS	*Journal of Theological Studies*
JUH	*Journal of Urban History*
Lat.	Latin
LCL	Loeb Classical Library
MHS	*Mental Health and Society*
NT	New Testament
NTTS	New Testament Tools and Studies
OBT	Overtures to Biblical Theology
OT	Old Testament
par.	parallel passages
PL	Patrologia latina
PLSup	Patrologia latina Supplement Series
PSS	*Philosophy of the Social Sciences*
SBEC	Studies in the Bible and Early Christianity
SBLDS	Society of Biblical Literature Dissertation Series
SNTSMS	Society for the Study of the New Testament Monograph Series

BIBLIOGRAPHY

Addinall, Peter. 1994. "Why Read the Bible? " *ExpT* 105:136–40.

Anderson, Benedict. 1991. *Imagined Communities: Reflections on the Origin and Spread of Nationalism*. London: Verso.

Augsburger, David W. 1986. *Pastoral Counseling Across Cultures*. Philadelphia: Westminster.

Auguet, Roland. [1972] 1994. *Cruelty and Civilization: The Roman Games*. Reprint, London: Routledge.

Bailey, F. G. 1970. *Stratagems and Spoils: A Social Anthropology of Politics*. Oxford: Blackwell.

Barr, James. 1988. "Abba Isn't 'Daddy.'" *JTS* 39:28–47.

Barton, Stephen C. 1992. "The Communal Dimension of Earliest Christianity: A Critical Survey of the Field." *JTS* 43: 399–427.

Barton, Stephen C. and Gregory H. R. Horsley. 1981. "A Hellenistic Cult Group and the New Testament Churches," *JAC* 24:7–41.

Black-Michaud, Jacob. 1975. *Cohesive Force: Feud in the Mediterranean and the Middle East*. New York: St. Martin's.

Block, Alan. 1983. *East Side West Side*. New Brunswick, N.J.: Transaction Books.

Blok, Anton. 1984. "Rams and Billy-Goats: a Key to the Mediterranean Code of Honour." Pp. 51–70 in Eric R. Wolf, ed. *Religion, Power and Protest in Local Communities: The Northern Shore of the Mediterranean*. Berlin: Mouton.

Boehm, Christopher. 1984. *Blood Revenge: The Anthropology of Feuding in Montenegro and Other Tribal Societies*. Lawrence: Univ. Press of Kansas.

Boissevain, Jeremy. 1974. *Friends of Friends: Networks, Manipulators and Coalitions*. New York: St. Martin's.

Breese, Gerald. 1966. *Urbanization in Newly Developing Countries.* Englewood Cliffs, N.J.: Prentice-Hall

Brenman, Eric. 1985. "Cruelty and Narrowmindedness." *IJP* 66:273–81.

Brown, Peter. 1978. *The Making of Late Antiquity.* Cambridge: Harvard Univ. Press.

Bultmann, Rudolf. 1963. *History of the Synoptic Tradition.* Trans. John Marsh. New York: Harper and Row.

Carney, Thomas F. 1973. *The Economies of Antiquity: Controls, Gifts and Trade.* Lawrence, Kans.: Coronado.

———. 1975. *The Shape of the Past: Models and Antiquity.* Lawrence, Kans.: Coronado.

Casson, Lionel. 1975. *Daily Life in Ancient Rome.* New York: American Heritage. Rev. ed. Baltimore: Johns Hopkins Univ. Press, 1999.

Charles, R. H. 1913. *Studies in the Apocalypse.* Edinburgh: T. & T. Clark; reprinted Eugene, Or.: Wipf and Stock, 1996.

Chilton, Bruce. 1994. "The Kingdom of God in Recent Discussion." Pp. 254–80 in Bruce Chilton and Craig A. Evans, eds. *Studying the Historical Jesus.* Leiden: Brill.

Cohn, Bernard S. 1980. "History and Anthropology: The State of Play." *CSSH* 22:198–221.

Collins, John J. 1983. *Between Athens and Jerusalem: Jewish Identity in the Hellenistic Diaspora.* New York: Crossroad.

Crick, Malcolm R. 1976. *Explorations in Language and Meaning: Towards a Semantic Anthropology.* London: Malaby.

Dalton, George. 1961. "Economic Theory and Primitive Society." *AmAnth* 63:3–25.

Duby, Georges and Philippe Braunstein. 1988. "The Emergence of the Individual." Pp. 507–630 in Georges Duby, ed. *A History of Private Life: II. Revelations of the Medieval World.* Trans. Arthur Goldhammer. Cambridge, Mass.: Belknap.

Dupont, Florence. 1992. *Daily Life in Ancient Rome.* Trans. Christopher Woodall. Oxford: Blackwell.

Eisenstadt, Shlomo N. 1963. *The Political Systems of Empires: The Rise and Fall of the Historical Bureaucratic Societies.* New York: Free Press.

Eisenstadt, Shlomo N. and Louis Roniger. 1984. *Patrons, Clients and Friends: Interpersonal Relations and the Structure of Trust in Society.* Cambridge: Cambridge Univ. Press.

Elliott, John H. 1990. *A Home for the Homeless: A Sociological Exegesis of 1 Peter, Its Situation and Strategy.* Rev. ed. Minneapolis: Fortress Press.

———. 1991. "Temple versus Household in Luke-Acts: A Contrast in Social Institutions." Pp. 211–40 in Jerome H. Neyrey, ed. *The Social World of Luke-Acts: Models for Interpretation.* Peabody, Mass.: Hendrickson.

———. 1994. *What is Social-Scientific Criticism?* GBS. Minneapolis: Fortress Press.

Esler, Philip F. 1987. *Community and Gospel in Luke-Acts: The Social and Political Motivations of Lucan Theology.* SNTSMS 57. New York: Cambridge Univ. Press.

Festugière, André-J. 1950. *La Révélation d'Hermès Trismégiste: Vol. I. L'Astrologie de les sciences occultes.* Paris: Gabalda.

Fiensy, David A. 1991. *The Social History of Palestine in the Herodian Period: This Land Is Mine.* Lewiston, N.Y.: Edwin Mellen.

Foster, George. 1965. "Peasant Society and the Image of Limited Good." *AmAnth* 67:293–315.

Foster, George M. 1972. "A Second Look at Limited Good." *AnthQ* 45: 57–64.

Fuellenbach, John. 1995. *The Kingdom of God: The Message of Jesus Today.* Maryknoll, N.Y.: Orbis.

Gallagher, Eugene V. 1982. *Divine Man or Magician? Celsus and Origen on Jesus.* SBLDS 64. Chico, Calif.: Scholars.

Gamson, William A. 1992. "The Social Psychology of Collective Action." Pp. 53–76 in Aldon D. Morris and Carol McClurg Mueller, eds. *Frontiers in Social Movement Theory.* New Haven: Yale Univ. Press.

Greene, Kevin. 1986. *The Archaeology of the Roman Economy.* Berkeley: Univ. of California Press.

Gregory, James R. 1975. "Image of Limited Good, or Expectation of Reciprocity?" *CurAnth* 16:73–92.

Gugler, Josef, ed. 1996. *The Urban Transformation of the Developing World.* Oxford: Oxford Univ. Press.

Guijarro, Santiago. 1997. "The Family in First-Century Galilee." Pp. 42–65 in Halvor Moxnes, ed. *Constructing Early Christian Families: Family as Social Reality and Metaphor.* London: Routledge.

Guijarro, Santiago. 1998. *Fidelidades en conflicto: La ruptura con la familia pro causa del discipulado y de la misión sinóptica.* Salamanca: Univ. Pontificia de Salamanca.

Hacquard, Georges, with J. Dautry and O. Maisani. 1952. *Guide Romain Antique.* Paris: Hachette.

Hall, Edward T. 1959. *The Silent Language.* Garden City: Doubleday.

———. 1976. *Beyond Culture.* Garden City, N.Y.: Doubleday.

———. 1983. *The Dance of Life: The Other Dimensions of Time.* Garden City, N.Y.: Doubleday.

Halliday, Michael A. K. 1978. *Language as Social Semiotic: The Social Interpretation of Language and Meaning.* Baltimore: University Park Press.

Hallie, Phillip P. 1982. *Cruelty.* Rev. ed. Middletown, Conn.: Wesleyan Univ. Press.

Hanson, K. C. 1989a. "The Herodians and Mediterranean Kinship: Part I: Genealogy and Descent." *BTB* 19:75–84.

———. 1989b. "The Herodians and Mediterranean Kinship: Part II: Marriage and Divorce." *BTB* 19:142–51.

———. 1990. "The Herodians and Mediterranean Kinship: Part III: Economics." *BTB* 20:10–21.

———. 1994. "BTB Readers Guide: Kinship." *BTB* 24:183–94.

Hanson, K. C. and Douglas Oakman. 1998. *Palestine in the Time of Jesus: Social Structures and Social Conflicts*. Minneapolis: Fortress Press.

Hays, Samuel P. 1993. "From the History of the City to the History of the Urbanized Society." *JUH* 19:3–25.

Hess, Henner. 1986. "The Traditional Sicilian Mafia: Organized Crime and Repressive Crime." Pp. 95–112 in Robert J. Kelly, ed. *Organized Crime: A Global Perspective*. Totowa, N.J.: Rowman & Littlefield.

Hofstede, Geert. 1980. *Cultures Consequences: International Differences in Work-Related Values*. Beverly Hills, Calif.: Sage.

———. 1994. *Cultures And Organizations: Software of The Mind: Intercultural Cooperation And Its Importance For Survival*. London: Harper Collins.

Hollenbach, Paul W. 1982a. "Jesus, Demoniacs, and Public Authorities: A Socio-Historical Study." *JAAR* 49:567–88.

———. 1982b. "The Conversion of Jesus: From Jesus the Baptizer to Jesus the Healer." *ANRW* II 25/1:196–219.

———. 1985. "Liberating Jesus for Social Involvement." *BTB* 15:151–57.

Hopkins, Keith. 1983. *Death and Renewal*. Sociological Studies in Roman History 2. Cambridge: Cambridge Univ. Press.

———. 1998. "Christian Number and Its Implications." *JECS* 6: 185–226.

Horsley, Richard A. 1988. *The Liberation of Christmas: The Infancy Narratives in Social Context*. New York: Crossroad.

———. 1994. *Sociology and the Jesus Movement*. 2nd ed. New York. Crossroad.

Horsley, Richard A. and John S. Hanson. 1985. *Bandits, Prophets, and Messiahs: Popular Movements at the Time of Jesus*. Minneapolis: Winston.

Humphreys, S. C. 1993. *The Family, Women and Death: Comparative Studies*. 2nd ed. Ann Arbor: Univ. of Michigan Press.

James, Paul. 1992. "Forms of Abstract 'Community': From Tribe and Kingdom to Nation and State." *PSS* 22: 313–36.

Judge, Edwin A. 1980. "The Social Identity of the First Christians: A Question of Method in Religious History." *JRH* 11:201–17.

Kautsky, John H. 1982. *The Politics of Aristocratic Empire.* Chapel Hill: Univ. of North Carolina Press.

Keen, Ian. 1985. "Definitions of Kin." *JAnthR* 41:62–90.

Kleijwegt, Marc. 1994. "'Voluntarily, But Under Pressure': Voluntarity and Constraint in Greek Municipal Politics." *Mnemosyne* 47: 64–78.

Landé, Carl H. 1977. "Introduction: The Dyadic Basis of Clientelism." Pp. xiii–xxxvii in Steffen W. Schmidt et al., eds., *Friends, Followers and Factions: A Reader in Political Clientelism.* Berkeley: Univ. of California Press,

Lowry, S. Todd. 1979. "Recent Literature on Ancient Greek Economic Thought." *JEL* 17:65–86.

Lupsha, Peter A. 1986. "Organized Crime in the United States." Pp. 32–57 in Robert J. Kelly, ed. *Organized Crime: A Global Perspective.* Totowa, N.J.: Rowman & Littlefield.

MacMullen, Ramsay. 1974. *Roman Social Relations: 50 B.C.. to A.D. 284.* New Haven: Yale Univ. Press.

———. 1981. *Paganism in the Roman Empire.* New Haven: Yale Univ. Press.

Malina, Bruce J. 1986a "'Religion' in the World of Paul." *BTB* 16:92–101.

———. 1986b *Christian Origins and Cultural Anthropology: Practical Models for Biblical Interpretation.* Atlanta: John Knox.

———. 1988. "Patron and Client: The Analogy Behind Synoptic Theology." *Forum* 4/1:2–32; reprinted pp. 143–75 in Bruce J. Malina, *The Social World of Jesus and the Gospels.* London: Routledge, 1996.

———. 1991a "Reading Theory Perspective: Reading Luke-Acts." Pp. 3–23 in Jerome H. Neyrey, ed. *The Social World of Luke-Acts: Models for Interpretation.* Peabody, Mass.: Hendrickson; reprinted pp. 3–31 in Bruce J. Malina. *The Social World of Jesus and the Gospels.* London: Routledge.

———. 1991b. "Interpretation: Reading, Abduction, Metaphor." Pp. 253–66 in David Jobling et al., eds. *The Bible and the Politics of Exegesis: Essays in Honor of Norman K. Gottwald on His Sixty-Fifth Birthday.* Cleveland: Pilgrim.

———. 1992. "Is There a Circum-Mediterranean Person? Looking for Stereotypes." *BTB* 22:66–87.

———. 1993. *The New Testament World: Insights from Cultural Anthropology.* Rev. ed. Louisville: Westminster John Knox.

———. 1994a. "Religion in the Imagined New Testament World: More Social Science Lenses." *Scriptura* 51:1–26.

———. 1994b. "'Let Him Deny Himself' (Mark 8:34//): A Social Psychological Model of Self-Denial." *BTB* 24:106–19.

———. 1995a. "Social Scientific Criticism and Rhetorical Criticism:

Why Won't Romanticism Leave Us Alone?" Pp. 71–101 in Stanley E. Porter and Thomas H. Olbricht, eds. *Rhetoric, Scripture and Theology: Essays from the. 1994 Pretoria Conference.* JSNTSup 131. Sheffield: Sheffield Academic Press.

————. 1995b. "Early Christian Groups: Using Small Group Formation Theory to Explain Christian Organizations." Pp. 143–75 in Philip F. Esler, ed. *Modelling Early Christianity: Social-Scientific Studies of the New Testament in its Context.* London: Routledge.

————. 1996a. "Mediterranean Sacrifice: Dimensions of Domestic and Political Religion." *BTB* 26:26–44.

————. 1996b. "Understanding New Testament Persons." Pp. 41–61 in Richard L. Rohrbaugh, ed. *The Social Sciences and New Testament Interpretation.* Peabody, Mass.: Hendrickson.

————. 1997a. "Embedded Economics: The Irrelevance of Christian Fictive Domestic Economy." *FSE* 26/2:1–20.

————. 1997b. "Mediterranean Cultural Anthropology and the New Testament." Pp. 151–78 in Augustí Borrell, Alfonson de la Fuente, and Armand Puig, eds. *La Bíblia i el Mediterrani—La Biblia y el Mediterráneo—La Bible et la Méditerranée—La Bibbia e il Mediterraneo.* (Actes del Congrés de Barcelona 18–22 de septembre de 1995). Vol. 1. Abadia de Montserrat: Associació Bíblica de Catalunya.

————. 1999. "Criteria for Assessing the Authentic Words of Jesus: Some Specifications." Pp. 27–45 in Craig A. Evans and Bruce Chilton, eds. *Authenticating the Words of Jesus.* NTTS 28/1 Leiden: Brill.

Malina, Bruce J. and Jerome H. Neyrey. 1996. *Portraits of Paul: An Archaeology of Ancient Personality.* Louisville: Westminster John Knox.

Malina, Bruce J. and Richard L. Rohrbaugh. 1993. *Social-Science Commentary on the Synoptic Gospels.* Minneapolis: Fortress Press.

————. 1998 *Social-Science Commentary on the Gospel of St. John.* Minneapolis: Fortress Press.

Mesnil, Michel. 1981. *L'uomo romano: uno studio di antropologia.* Milan: Mondadori.

McCarthy, John D. and Mayer N. Zald. 1987. "Resource Mobilization and Social Movements: A Partial Theory." Pp. 15–42 in Mayer N. Zald and John D. McCarthy, eds. *Social Movements in an Organizational Society.* New Brunswick, N.J.: Transactions Books.

Messick, David M. and Diane M. Mackie. 1989. "Intergroup Relations." *ARP* 40:45–81.

Millar, Fergus. 1977. *The Emperor in the Roman World, 31 BC–AD 337,* Ithaca, N.Y.: Cornell Univ. Press.

Miller, John. 1997. *Jesus at Thirty: A Psychological and History Study.* Minneapolis: Fortress Press.

Moreland, Richard L. and John M. Levine. 1988. "Group Dynamics Over Time: Development and Socialization in Small Groups." Pp. 151–81 in Joseph E. McGrath, ed. *The Social Psychology of Time: New Perspectives.* Newbury Park, Calif.: Sage.

Morris, Brian. 1987. *Anthropological Studies of Religion: An Introductory Text.* Cambridge: Cambridge Univ. Press.

Moxnes, Halvor. 1988. *The Economy of the Kingdom: Social Conflict and Economic Relations in Luke's Gospel.* OBT. Philadelphia: Fortress Press.

———. 1991. "Patron-Client Relations and the New Community in Luke-Acts." Pp. 241–71 in Jerome H. Neyrey, ed. *The Social World of Luke-Acts: Models for Interpretation.* Peabody, Mass.: Hendrickson.

———. 1997. "What is Family? Problems in Constructing Early Christian Families." Pp. 13–41 in Halvor Moxnes, ed. *Constructing Early Christian Families: Family as Social Reality and Metaphor.* London: Routledge.

Mullin, Redmond. 1984. *The Wealth of Christians.* Maryknoll, N.Y.: Orbis.

Neyrey, Jerome H. 1998. *Honor and Shame in the Gospel of Matthew.* Louisville: Westminster John Knox.

Oakman, Douglas E. 1991. "The Countryside in Luke-Acts." Pp. 151–79 in Jerome H. Neyrey, ed. *The Social World of Luke-Acts: Models for Interpretation.* Peabody, Mass.: Hendrickson.

———. 1985. *Jesus and the Economic Questions of His Day.* Lewiston, N.Y.: Edwin Mellen.

Parsons, Talcott 1960. *Structure and Process in Modern Societies.* New York: Free Press, 1960.

Pilch, John J. 1993a. "'Beat His Ribs While He Is Young' (Sir 30:12): A Window on the Mediterranean World." *BTB* 23:101–13.

———. 1993b. "Visions in Revelation and Alternate Consciousness: A Perspective from Cultural Anthropology." *Listening* 28:231–44.

———. 1997. "Psychological and Psychoanalytical Approaches to Interpreting the Bible in Social-Scientific Context." *BTB* 27:112–16.

Pitt-Rivers, Julian. 1968 "Pseudo-Kinship." Pp. 408–13 in David L. Sills ed. *International Encyclopedia of the Social Sciences* 8. New York: Macmillan and The Free Press.

Polanyi, Karl. 1968 *Primitive, Archaic and Modern Economies: Essays of Karl Polanyi.* George Dalton, ed. Boston: Beacon.

Powell, John Duncan. "Peasant Society and Clientelistic Politics." Pp. 147–61 in Schmidt, et al.

Rohrbaugh, Richard L. 1991. "The Pre-Industrial City in Luke-Acts: Urban Social Relations." Pp. 125–49 in Jerome H. Neyrey, ed. *The Social World of Luke-Acts: Models for Interpretation.* Peabody, Mass.: Hendrickson.

Rosenbaum, M. E., *et multi alii*. 1988. "Group Productivity and Process: Pure and Mixed Reward Structures and Task Interdependence." *JPSP* 39:626–42.

Ross, Robert and Staines, Graham L. 1972. "The Politics of Analyzing Social Problems." *Social Problems* 20:18–40.

Rothenberger, John E. 1978. "The Social Dynamics of Dispute Settlement in a Sunni Muslim Village in Lebanon." Pp. 152–80 in Laura Nader and Harry F. Todd Jr., eds. *The Disputing Process—Law in Ten Societies*. New York: Columbia Univ. Press.

Rouland, Norbert. 1979. *Pouvoir politique et dépendance personnelle dans l'Antiquité romaine: Génèse et role des relations de clientèle*. Bruxelles: Latomus.

Routledge, Bruce. 1997. "Learning to Love the King: Urbanism and the State in Iron Age Moab." Pp 130–44 in Walter E. Aufrecht, Neil A. Mirau, and Steven W. Gauley, eds. *Urbanism in Antiquity: From Mesopotamia to Crete*. JSOTSup 244. Sheffield: Sheffield Academic.

Rupp, David W. 1997. "'Metro' Nea Paphos: Suburban Sprawl in Southwestern Cyprus in the Hellenistic and Earlier Roman Periods." Pp. 236–62 in Walter E. Aufrecht, Neil A. Mirau, and Steven W. Gauley, eds. *Urbanism in Antiquity: From Mesopotamia to Crete*. JSOTSup 244. Sheffield: Sheffield Academic.

Sack, Robert David. 1986. *Human Territoriality: Its Theory and History*. Cambridge Studies in Historical Geography. Cambridge: Cambridge Univ. Press.

Saller, Richard P. 1982. *Personal Patronage Under the Early Empire*. Cambridge: Cambridge Univ. Press.

———. 1984. "Familia, Domus, and the Roman Conception of the Family." *Phoenix* 38:336–55.

Southall, Aidan. 1998. *The City in Time and Space*. Cambridge: Cambridge Univ. Press.

Stegemann, Wolfgang. 1984. *The Gospel and the Poor*. Trans. D. Elliott. Philadelphia: Fortress Press.

Stevenson, T. R. 1992. "The Ideal Benefactor and the Father Analogy in Greek and Roman Thought." *CQ* 42/2:421–36

Sweeney, Ernest S. 1984. "The Nature and Power of Religion in Latin America: Some Aspects of Popular Beliefs and Practices." *Thought* 59:149–63.

Taylor, Lily Ross. 1961. *Party Politics in the Age of Caesar*. Berkeley: Univ. of California Press.

———. 1977. "Nobles, Clients and Personal Armies." Pp. 179–92 in Schmidt et al.

Terrenato, Nicola. 1998. "Tam Firmum Municipium: The Romanization of Volaterrae and Its Cultural Implications." *JRS* 88:94–114.

Triandis, Harry C. 1989. "Cross-Cultural Studies of Individualism and Collectivism" Pp. 41–133 in Richard A. Dienstbier, et al., eds. *Nebraska Symposium on Motivation.* Lincoln: Univ. of Nebraska Press.

Tuckman, B. W. 1965. "Developmental Sequence in Small Groups." *Psychological Bulletin* 63:384–99.

Turner, Jonathan H., with A. Maryanski and Stephan Fuchs. 1991. *The Structure of Sociological Theory.* 5th ed. Belmont, Calif.: Wadsworth.

Verdon, Michel. 1981. "Kinship, Marriage and the Family: An Operational Approach," *AJS* 86:796–818.

Veyne, Paul. 1976 *Le Pain et Le Cirque: Sociologie Historique d'un Pluralisme Politique.* Paris: du Seuil.

———. 1989. "'Humanitas': Romani e no[i]." Pp. 385–415 in Andrea Giardina, ed. *L'uomo Romano.* Bari: Laterza.

———. 1998. "Rome: Une Société d'hommes." *L'Histoire* 221 (May): 37.

Veyne, Paul ed. 1987. *A History of a Private Life, Vol. I: From Pagan Rome to Byzantium.* Trans. Arthur Goldhammer. Cambridge, Mass.: Belknap.

Wallace-Hadrill, Andrew, ed. 1990. *Patronage in Ancient Society.* Leicester-Nottingham Studies in Ancient Society 1. London: Routledge.

Walston, James. 1986. "See Naples and Die: Organized Crime in Campania." Pp. 134–58 in Robert J. Kelly, ed. *Organized Crime: A Global Perspective.* Totowa, N.J.: Rowman & Littlefield.

Walters, Glenn D. 1990. *The Criminal Lifestyle: Patterns of Serious Criminal Conduct.* Newbury Park, Calif.: Sage.

Weaver, P. R. C. 1972. *Familia Caesaris: A Social Study of the Emperor's Freedmen and Slaves.* Cambridge: Cambridge Univ. Press.

White, L. Michael. 1982. *Domus Ecclesiae—Domus Dei: Adaptation and Development in the Setting for Early Christian Assembly.* Ann Arbor: University Microfilms International; Yale Univ. Dissertation.

Wilken, Robert L. 1971. "Collegia, Philosophical Schools, and Theology." Pp. 268–91 in Stephen Benko and John J. O'Rourke, eds. *The Catacombs and the Colosseum: The Roman Empire as the Setting of Primitive Christianity.* Valley Forge, Pa.: Judson.

Willis, W. ed. 1987. *The Kingdom of God in 20th-century Interpretation.* Peabody, Mass.: Hendrickson.

Wilson, Bryan. 1975. *Magic and the Millennium: A Sociological Study of Religious Movements of Protest among Tribal and Third-World Peoples.* St. Albans, England: Paladin.

Worsley, Peter. 1984. *The Three Worlds: Culture and World Development.* Chicago: Univ. of Chicago Press.

Zald, Mayer N. and John D. McCarthy. 1987. "Religious Groups as Crucibles of Social Movements." Pp. 67–95 in Mayer N. Zald and John D. McCarthy, eds. *Social Movements in an Organizational Society*, New Brunswick, N.J.: Transactions Books.

Zander, Alvin. 1971. *Motives and Goals in Groups*. Orlando: Academic.

———. 1985. *The Purposes of Groups and Organizations*. San Francisco: Jossey-Bass.

Index of Ancient Sources

ᏮᏞᎧ INDEX OF ANCIENT SOURCES

2 Corinthians

6:10	98
8:9	98, 105
9:8	109
9:9	98
11:12	40

Galatians

1:15-16	145
2:7-9	154
2:10	98
3:1	105
3:28	49
4:6	142
4:14	105
5:21	159
6:10	159

Ephesians

2:4	98
5:5	159

Philippians

4:11	109

Colossians

3:11	49

1 Thessalonians

2:12	159
4:12	109

1 Timothy

5:18	81
6:6	109
6:10	100
6:17	100

2 Timothy

3:1-4	100

Hebrews

9:7—10:20	40
12:4, 24	40
12:5-7	40
13:11-12, 20	40

James

1:10-11	100
2:3-6	99
2:6-7	100
5:1-7	100

Revelation

1:3, 10	145
2:9	98
3:17-18	100
3:17	99
6:15	100
13:16	98
18:3, 15, 18	100

ANCIENT AUTHORS

Aristotle
Politics III, 9 1256b
104
Politics III, 12–20
1257a–1258a
110
Politics III, 16 1257b
106

Clement of Alexandria
Paidagogos, II, 14, 5
106

Council of Carthage
401   109

Diodorus Siculus, 30

Gospel of Thomas

55	115
90	116
101	115

Jerome
Epistle 120:
to Hedebia   106

In Hieremiam, II,V,2
106
Tract. de Ps LXXXIII,
lines 29–30   106

Menander (frag.) 129,
294   106

Philo
Embassy to Gaius, 54

145	49
147	49

*On Rewards and Pun-
ishments* 168   107
Special Laws

1.315–17	41
1.54	41
2., 122	110
4:195–96	99

Plato
Laws, 12, 743   106

Plutarch
On Love of Wealth,

523F	106
525-526	108
528A	110

Sayings of Spartans
226D   17
Table Talk V 5 679 A-C
108

Pseudo-Pelagius
On Wealth II   107
XX,4   107

Seneca
Epistle 17, 9   106

Strabo
Geography 1.4.9   49